"Nice? It's the only thing," said the Water Rat, solemnly, as he leant forward for his stroke. *"Believe me, my young friend, there is nothing—absolutely nothing—half so much worth doing as simply messing about in boats. Simply mess-ing,"* he went on dreamily: *"messing—about—in—boats; messing—"*

From *The Wind in the Willows* by Kenneth Grahame.
By courtesy of Methuen & Co., Limited.

My home for eight years

MESSING ABOUT
IN BOATS

SURGEON REAR ADMIRAL
John R. Muir
M.B., F.R.C.S.E.

Lodestar Books

First published 1938 by Blackie and Son
This edition published 2016 by
Lodestar Books
71 Boveney Road, London, SE23 3NL, United Kingdom

www.lodestarbooks.com

A CIP catalogue record for this book
is available from the British Library

ISBN 978-1-907206-38-2

Typeset by Lodestar Books in Equity

Printed in Spain by Graphy Cems, Navarra

All papers used by Lodestar Books
are sourced responsibly

Contents

To My Wife

Foreword

THERE WAS A MAN IN THE VILLAGE who used to come and do a bit of stone-work round and about the house. I was talking to him one day, and he vouchsafed the information that he had spent five years in the Navy. I asked him where he had been. He looked puzzled. 'I dunno,' he said. 'I didn't go outdoors much.'

This was not the approach of Surgeon Rear Admiral Muir. No sooner had a Naval tour of duty finished and a leave started than he would be shooting off to whatever yacht held his fancy at that moment. One of the joys of this memoir is that in an era when yachting was a rich man's pursuit, at least in the early stages of his life he managed the whole business on his pay—a model for the many Minimum Boat owners stretching their finances to cracking-point to mess around on the sea.

His stories come from another (some would say infintely more interesting) era. Some have a powerful resonance today. Conned by longshore brutes, the yacht brokers of his time, he buys boats notable for their rottenness and furbishes them up himself. Others of his stories are period pieces. In an era where weather forecasting was even less exact than it is now he rode out plenty of gales, mingling at times with the North Sea fishing fleets, and learning in the process an admiration for the seamanship of working mariners. In a world divided between gentlemen and players he paid little attention to the class divide. At first this meant treating his paid hands as human beings rather than cyphers, and understanding (if not sympathising with) their fallibilities in the matter of strong drink and personal hygiene. It reached a sort of zenith when he conceived the idea that a Bristol Channel pilot cutter, by the standards of his age a somewhat *infra dig* working boat, could be considered as a possible yacht. As part of researching this notion, he took the then extraordinary step of signing on as a paid hand on one of them, spending a good stretch of a winter leave putting up with anything the Bristol Channel could throw at him in the way of frost, gales and five-knot tides.

Above all, this is a book that reflects a life shot through with the love of the sea and sailing. When you read it, you will be reassured (if reassurance is needed) of the great truth uttered by Ratty in *The Wind in the Willows* and quoted in this book's title: there is nothing, simply nothing, half so much worth doing.

Sam Llewellyn
September 2016

I

My First Yacht

A LTHOUGH AT THE AGE OF THIRTEEN my father had presented me with my first thirteen-foot sailing boat, it was not until nearly six years later that I became possessed of my first real, decked, sea-going yacht. The thirteen-foot dinghy had taught me something of sailing, as she was a heavily built craft of the ship's boat type, rigged with the now almost obsolete sprit-sail and jib. She took some handling, but in her I had sailed all round the islands of Grenada and the Grenadines, having on one occasion adventured as far as Cariacou.

Usually I was chaperoned by an aged negro servant who had actually been born a slave. His function was to act as motive power in a calm, but if I could dodge him I always dispensed with his services as he suffered from epilepsy. If there was any particularly exciting work, and excitement comes quickly in the Caribbean Sea, he invariably chose that moment to chuck a fit.

I learned all that could be learned in the way of sailing and handling a rather clumsy open boat in rough weather, and in various of the local sloops I had done quite a lot of surreptitious sailing, so that I considered myself fairly expert. But after I came home to school in Scotland I had no opportunities of getting any experience in other sailing craft, much though I longed to do so. Of course there was always the *Boys' Own Paper* with Frank Cowper's articles to keep the hidden fires burning, and well they fed the flame.

I saw her first with a broom at her masthead lying amongst a crowd of derelicts in a forgotten corner of Leith docks. I had been wandering round that May afternoon, full of envy and longing, watching every movement on the big and small sailing ships—and they had real sailing ships in those days ranging from the huge 3000-ton steel four-posters to the little wooden brigs and schooners which brought timber from the Baltic, but the sight of this broom and its well-known significance were too much for me to let me pass along. I looked at the hull under the broom and the little ship looked like a queen among a crowd of kitchen sluts—all due to a coat of fresh paint slapped on by the wily seller in order to lure a purchaser, but with a heart beating to suffocation I clambered across the intervening vessels and went on board.

She seemed to be the size I imagined I could manage single-handed, and, as she was not locked up, it was possible to examine her accommodation, which was satisfactory—that is to say there was room to sit up and to lie down. The next thing to do was to find the owner and that was easy as he was the foreman rigger in a local yard and was working on board one of the nearby vessels.

I hunted him up, and back we came together to the ship, where we sat in the little saloon whilst he expatiated on all her good points and, diplomatically, ignored her bad ones. But what I wanted to know most of all was her price, and he was heartbreakingly slow in coming to that answer to my eager questioning. At last it came out, and when he said that it was a gift at £25 my heart sank into my boots. I scarcely know what I expected him to say. The son of a poor Scots parson being trained as a medical student has no business with yachts. He should be getting on with the work and not dreaming of sailing over summer seas and stealing away from quaint harbours at dawn. How to raise this £25 was a quandary indeed. But I had a goodly share of spare time on my hands during the summer, and I had to live somewhere during that period and I believed I could do it even more cheaply than by inflicting myself on unwilling friends if I lived on board the yacht. My father used to send me an extra £10 for the holiday period. I had a very good microscope which I could pawn. I could go short of a lot of things. I could—well, I could do desperate things to have a yacht, and was going to do them.

So a bargain at £22 was struck with the rigger, and I handed over £2 (they were golden sovereigns and very precious in those days) as earnest money with the agreement that the yacht was to be out of the docks and lying in Leith harbour, ready to sail for Granton on the following Saturday when the purchase would be completed.

I raised the money—how I hardly know. I remember a very desperate youngster standing in the pawnbroker's shop insisting on being allowed £7 on a microscope which the broker swore was worth only £5, and getting it by sheer persistence. I kept my divinity student brother out of bed the whole of one night while I begged and prayed him to lend me some money he had saved up for his own holiday—and got it. I went without lunch at the Union for the rest of the time I owned the boat, saving thereby about five shillings a week. And there was endless juggling with clothes and cheaper rooms so that I might be enabled to join the monied classes and become the owner of a yacht without owing a penny to anyone.

And the yacht! A feeling of awe used to come over me as I whispered her name in the night watches. *Orion*! The same name as McMullen's famous ship! She had a counter and a straight stem; black topsides and red anti-fouling below the water-line; a good outfit of sails and rigging (trust the rigger to look out for that); a real saloon and a tiny forecastle where two could sleep, but only after a heated discussion over which of the two was to be allowed to stretch himself out. She had a big well and was twenty-eight feet overall, twenty-three feet on the water-line, eight feet beam and drew five feet. Even in the year of grace of 1892 she was old-fashioned looking, and her history went back to the remote 'fifties. She had been a schooner and a yawl, but when I bought her she was rigged as a cutter. Her inventory was chiefly conspicuous for the absence of sea-going gear, and the below furnishing was beneath contempt. A one-burner Beatrice stove, a tin kettle, and a stewpan represented her galley on the forecastle floor, whilst the saloon was lit by a sixpenny wall lamp. There was a hopeless box compass (which nevertheless took me to the Texel and through the Pentland Firth) and her cable was partly a length of coir and partly a coil of wire rope. The rest of the fit-out, with the exception of the running rigging, was in keeping and no more need be said about it. Her one glory was a pair of beautifully carved and polished mahogany panels at the back of the saloon settees.

But she represented to me the romance and freedom of the seas, and the day I stepped on board her as her owner I would not have exchanged her for the finest new product of the builder's yard, paid for by the soulless writing of a careless cheque. The rigger had brought one of his underlings to help and between us we navigated her to Granton which was the only place suitable as headquarters. We arrived there of course after I had been covered with confusion again and again by the two experts and had lost most of the skin of the palm of my hand because I insisted on holding the fall of the main-sheet dinghy fashion. The rigger was kindly, but not much interested or enthusiastic about my joyous confidences as to the glorious future I was planning for the ship and myself. The underling sat on the bowsprit bitts in order to attend to the head-sheets, but did not open his mouth to make any remark until we had anchored and everything had been stowed away. Then, just as he was leaving me to the bliss of sole ownership, he approached me and said in a gruff undertone: 'The topsail halyards is rove, sir!'

I knew the significance of the statement that the sun is over the foreyard and guessed that there might be some hidden meaning in this apparently harmless information. So one of my last half-crowns unobtrusively changed ownership and was stealthily secreted. Gratified, apparently, by the readiness of my comprehension the hand went on still in a hoarse whisper: 'Don't you spend any money on her. She isn't worth it. She's rotten!' and went over the side, shaking his head lugubriously. Of course I labelled him a liar who had some grievance against his foreman. I had no doubt that he was also deeply envious of me and my new possession and was disgruntled. Anyhow, I had got a yacht and that kind of remark went out of my mind at once, only to be recalled in later days when I found how moderate his statement was compared to the real state of affairs.

After much cogitation and pocket-searching I had joined a local Yacht Club, so as to avoid the expense of my own moorings, have somewhere to leave my dinghy, and to be able to claim one of their casual hands who were available to assist members when required. For my first week-end sail I slept (or didn't sleep through excitement) in the saloon, one of the said hands occupying the forecastle so that we could get away at dawn. The commissariat was generous, consisting of tea, sugar, condensed milk, two loaves, some butter, two tins of soup, and a two-gallon jar of water. But the hand did not seem to think much of my catering and querulously pointed out the value of whisky in case we got wet. But whisky was three shillings a bottle and therefore, for me at any rate, an impossible sybaritic luxury.

The east-going tide would serve at 4 a.m., and shortly before that hour I routed out the sleepy-head who had come on board very late the evening before, after leaving me to my supper of soup and bread and butter. His first remark on my projected sail to Elie was that the wind didn't suit, and that to get there in one tide was impossible. I deferred to his superior knowledge of the ways of the Firth of Forth, and suggested in that case we could sail to Charleston in the opposite direction. This was met with the objection that the tide didn't suit—which was perfectly true. I had sense enough to know that if I wanted to do any sailing in British waters I could hardly expect the wind and tide to agree to be always in my favour, and began to fear that I was going to miss my sail altogether. So summoning up all my hardihood I faced this bearded ruffian and said that in my opinion it was he himself who did not suit. He thought himself secure in the belief that I could not sail without him, but by 4 a.m. he was standing on the East breakwater and I was doing my best to remember exactly how my rigger and his mate had got the canvas on her.

By the mercy of that providence at sea which watches over fools and bairns, I arrived at Elie and anchored off the pier in such a position that if an on-shore breeze had sprung up I must inevitably have been wrecked. But I escaped scatheless, and in due time picked up my moorings at Granton by the simple expedient of drifting down on top of them. I did not understand the hand's action until later when I heard that his idea of a week-end sail was to cross to Aberdour about five miles away, dry out against the wall of the little harbour, spend the night there and sail back the next day.

That was my first attempt at single-handed sailing, over 100 miles, but there were many other days and nights of adventure afterwards—the night I lay to, my sunken dinghy as a sea-anchor, with my body wedged between the cabin settees as the only place to find rest, and also because I knew when my shoulders got wet it was time to get up and pump: the night I wandered uneasily up and down the deck of a fishing smack, somewhere off the Dogger, because I had been frightened by the awful forebodings of the kindly crew and had tied *Orion* astern of her while the smack rode out the gale to her trawl, the days when I drifted down the Forth to meet a strong easterly breeze close to North Berwick, and was driving on to the Gullane sands because I could neither make her stay nor wear and finally got her about by letting go my kedge and losing it over the stern: when I put about off the Texel nine days out from Granton, bound to go straight back if I were to be able to sit for a professional examination: when I went through the Pentland Firth stern first, although there was plenty of wind and the Merry Men of Mey were howling their delight at my approach.

But I was learning, and as Jack London remarked, 'Learning even better than I knew.' I learned that a shiny black hull and a beautiful red bottom can cover a multitude of defects hopeless of remedy, and that when a boat 'leaked enough to keep her sweet' she was a sink for money and beyond all repair. I learned that he who puts to sea with rotten gear will surely rue his rashness if life be granted him in which to do so; that the kindly sea is no respecter of the blue serge suit, or the compendium of nautical language; that it tolerates the errors of the willing learner, but shows no mercy to the expert; that the price of safety is eternal vigilance; that the sea labourer must never be confounded with the seaman; that the sea is in all circumstances safer than the land whether boat or man is concerned.

But, above all, I learned that 'Who hath desired the sea and her excellent loneliness' will never until the day of his death be content with aught else.

II

In the North Sea

TOWARDS THE END OF LAST CENTURY I had come up to London to grind for the entrance examination for the Royal Navy which was usually held in October. As that month passed and the customary advertisement did not appear, I wrote to the Admiralty to ask when I would be expected to sit, only to learn that there would be no opportunity until February. My depleted exchequer did not justify so prolonged a period of idleness, and I was puzzled how to fill up the interval until I saw a notice in one of the medical journals that a surgeon was required for an indefinite period on board the mission ship *Clulow*, belonging to the Royal National Mission to Deep Sea Fishermen. There must have been a shortage of applicants for the job—presumably the season of the year had something to do with that—for I received an appointment and was given instructions how to join the ship, which was attached to the Great Northern Fishing Fleet, at that time working in some unspecified area in the North Sea. The orders were to board, at a wharf at Billingsgate, a vessel known as a fish carrier and report myself to the skipper, who had been warned to expect me and would do the rest. The letter tactfully hinted that an early interview with the steward, and the surreptitious passage from my palm to an expectant one of some loose coin of the realm, was calculated to add to the pleasure of all concerned in the trip.

There was a false move at the start because I hired a hansom (this was in the nineties called 'naughty', though at the time I was completely ignorant of the terrible cloud under which my youth was being passed), and it took three repetitions of my destination before I could get Jehu to believe that I was not making him the subject of an ill-timed jest at seven in the morning. He admitted, when convinced that I was serious, that he had only the vaguest notion of the locality and, when I chaffed him about his meagre knowledge, told me roundly that a growler was more in my line than a hansom, whose usual beat was confined to the West End. In those days only inferiority complexes and maiden aunts patronized growlers, and at first I shrank from this degradation, but Jehu insisted that if I wanted to arrive in time a growler it would have to be, and I gave in. The vehicle with its bottle-nosed driver was produced, my luggage loaded on top, I entered the smelly interior and, feeling like a rabbit in a hutch, made a tedious journey to the wharf. The ship was lying alongside with steam up and only waiting for my arrival to shove off. Being of an obedient disposition I at once sought an interview with the steward, whose unwashed and unshaven face became wreathed in smiles as a small golden coin changed ownership. The Mission had already paid handsomely for my passage, so that this cruising liner was no further expense to me.

No sooner was I on board than the skipper jumped up from his bunk in his cabin, pulled on his sea-boots—the only toilet he ever indulged in while I was on board the ship—went to the wheel, rang up the engine-room, cast off his warps and pushed off into the muddy stream. I knew the Thames intimately from London Bridge to Orford Ness, and this part of the journey provided no novelty, so I passed the time during the voyage to Gravesend in taking stock of the ship, which, according to my friend the steward, might be my home for a week or more.

Except that they were a little bigger and were not usually fitted with trawling gear, these carriers were much the same in appearance as any of the other steam vessels that fish in the North Sea. Their special duty was to bring the fish from the trawling fleet to the market, and consequently they had a larger hold capacity than the true trawler, and they also carried large stores of ice for the preservation of the fish. A favourite joke was to tell of the housewife who refused to buy fish on Mondays because fishermen did not work on Sundays, and therefore the fish could not possibly be fresh. Before I left the fleet I appreciated that joke as much as any of them, for the complete ignorance it betrayed of the conditions under which fish are supplied.

The particular ship which was proceeding on her malodorous way with me as passenger had a high, sheering fo'c'sle head under which five of her crew of ten had their berths. Aft of this was an enormous fore well-deck almost entirely occupied by the hatches that protected the fish hold. This was succeeded by the fiddley, an iron superstructure over the engine-room and stokehold. Perched above the fore end of the fiddley was the tiny wheelhouse, while in the after end was the galley, through which one passed to the ladder leading to the saloon and skipper's cabin down below in the stern. The small boat was in chocks over the saloon skylight, in such a position that the skylight, our only means of direct ventilation, could not be opened, and was almost useless for lighting purposes. I was told that the fishermen preferred the boat in this awkward place as it saved the skylight from being smashed by a sea coming over aft. The ship was rigged as a ketch, the foremast in a tabernacle having no sail set, while the mizen-mast was fixed and had the sail constantly set. In my opinion that sail was so stiff from saturation with soot that it was well-nigh impossible to stow it. The wheel was connected up with the tiller quadrant aft by means of loose chains, which clanked amazingly on the bare steel deck at every movement of the wheel. Her engines drove her at a speed of about ten knots, although her chief engineer lived on the memory of the twelve she did on her trials. He was a retired engine-room artificer from the Navy, and, when he knew where my ambitions were leading me, gave me much inside information about the quality of the food which was served out to the lower deck in Her Majesty's ships and vessels.

On descending the ladder from the galley one arrived in a large alleyway to port, with the captain's cabin, entered from the saloon, to starboard. The lobby was encroached upon by storerooms. The saloon was furnished with a large semi-circular table surrounded by a settee aft, and a huge coal stove against the forrard bulkhead, which was about six feet away from the straight edge of the table and gave the only foot room in the cabin. On the starboard side of this bulkhead was the entrance to the dog-kennel which was the skipper's cabin. Behind the settee in the saloon were four box bunks, two on each side, occupied by the mate, steward, bo'sun and engineer. The mate, one of the finest looking men I have ever met, offered me the use of his berth for the duration of my stay. I refused, saying that I would be quite comfortable on the settee, and anyway, I, an idle individual, was not going to deprive a hard-working man of his bed. His reply was illuminating, 'Well, I don't know but what you are right. Sometimes it's that lively I can hardly stay in it myself, and I don't think you could unless you was used to them things.'

It was a dull winter's day outside, and the only light below had been filtered through some dirty deck prisms so that my effort at reading a paper was a failure. Seeing the fix I was in, the steward lit the acetylene gas jets. The stove was already roaring up the chimney, and these lights added so much to the temperature of the saloon that I got up and fled after eating for lunch such fish as never, in its supreme excellence, appears on the tables of a fashionable restaurant. The ship was nearing Gravesend, where we were to fill up with coal and ice. We went to the collier first and then to the ice hulk. These operations were not completed until after dark, so we stood off a bit and anchored for the night. Our bunkers were full and there were stacks of coal on deck between the fiddley and the bulwarks. We were to start early in the morning; but in the meantime no effort was made to wash down the ship, and we sat at supper as we were, begrimed with coal-dust, with the whole of the furniture covered with a thin film of carbon. The ventilation, i.e., the doorway of the galley, had been carefully kept shut when coaling but, although it had prevented the ingress of air most efficiently, it had been powerless to exclude the halo of coal-dust in which we had been enveloped for three hours.

I had donned an old suit of clothes for the coaling, and after supper suggested to the steward that it would be pleasant if I could have a bath and then shift into clean clothes. He said he could arrange the bath, and late in the evening a huge zinc tub was put on the floor in front of the stove and filled with hot water. The mate, having heard a rumour of these strange proceedings, came below to investigate, sat down on the settee, and lit his pipe with the air of a man who was going to have a novel form of entertainment provided for his special benefit. He said that he had heard from the steward I was going to have a bath; that he did not bother much about that sort of thing himself as washing always gave him a cold; but that his missus was a holy terror, and made the lives of himself and the children a misery with her ideas on this debatable subject. He had no false modesty about leaving me to get on with my bath, and I could hardly turn him out, so there was nothing to be done but strip in front of him. The result to him was the most astonishing feature of the whole performance. He got up from his seat and, pointing the stem of his pipe at me, exclaimed: 'Man, you're clean! What do ye want with a bath? All ye want to do is to give your hands and face a bit of a wipe.' However, in spite of his protests, I finished my bath and, incidentally, provided the skipper and him with a subject for prolonged and animated discussion as long as I remained in the ship. But I did not repeat the experiment. Water is at a premium in the North Sea, and not to be lightly wasted in a work of supererogation such as washing.

With a travelling rug over me and a Gladstone bag under my head for a pillow I spent a restless night on the hard settee. The others in the box bunks were equally restless, for a multitude of reasons with which I am glad to say I had no personal contact. I think we were all glad when we heard the skipper pulling on his boots just before dawn. The morning toilet of the rest of us was not any more complicated, and as we passed through the galley on our way to the deck the steward handed each of us a mug of tea which had been prepared for duty by stewing on top of the red hot stove all night. It was as black as ink and only rendered palatable by being made almost syrupy with sugar. At the time it struck me as being almost as potent as any dope. This milk-less beverage was handed out at all hours of the day or night, and it was rare to see the skipper without a mug on the shelf in the wheel-house.

The skipper asked me to come with him, and we climbed into the wheel-house, where I crushed myself into a corner while he leant out of the forward window and, with a wave of his mug, indicated to the mate on the fo'c'sle head the direction in which he proposed to turn the ship in order to proceed down stream. Vessels of all sizes were passing up and down, big sailing ships were being towed seaward, and numberless barges and bawleys obstructed the channel. Most of the steamers, like the motorist of later days, seemed to think that noise was a sufficient substitute for skilful handling, and the row from their sirens and foghorns was deafening. Something more than moderate skill was required to get the fish carrier safely into a place in the descending procession and join the outflow that the ebb was hurrying out to sea. It was a scene that in its infinite variety of ships has passed away for ever, but I am glad to have lived and seen it. We dodged amongst the lot of them down the lower reaches of the river, and when we had picked up the Mouse, altered course for the Swin, so that late in the evening we said goodbye to the coast of England as Orford Ness disappeared in the haze of a November sunset.

I had stayed in the wheelhouse all day as the decks were so littered with coal that movement was difficult, but the stokers were working on the deck cargo, and I learned that in a day or two it would be all burned, and a few odd seas were confidently awaited to finish the job of washing down. In time both hopes were fulfilled, but meanwhile we were heading out to sea, and I had not the foggiest notion where we were bound, though the compass showed that our course was north-east. Experience had taught me that it was easy to become very unpopular by asking when you were likely to arrive at your destination. Seamen in those days still laboured under the uncertainties of the old sailing ship passages, and heartily disliked being asked to commit themselves to a definite statement. On the strength of our long day together I risked a snub and asked meekly where the skipper had left the fishing fleet a week before. He replied at once that he had left them somewhere off the Horns reef near the coast of Jutland, but that he had no doubt they had left that fishing ground, though where they had gone to he had no idea. The only thing to do was to search for them, and that might take a week or more. It sounded rather haphazard, so I asked how he proposed to look for them. He explained that one carrier left the fleet every day, unless the weather was so bad that they were unable to fill up, and that on his present course he was bound to meet one of them on the way in, and they would give him the latest information. And that was precisely how we did it. For four days we literally asked our way and, late one evening, got information that the fleet was about thirty miles away in a north-west direction. We headed for them, and about ten o'clock the skipper called my attention to a rocket bursting in the sky. He was confident that it was from our fleet and was a signal from the Admiral to shoot the trawls. After straining our eyes for some time they suddenly came into view through some low-lying haze. They were a wonderful sight. We were heading straight for the middle of a crescent of fifty trawlers all steaming slowly to windward and keeping perfect station on the Admiral, whose ship was the centre of the crescent. Their steaming lights, a red, white and green lantern at the masthead with an all-round white light below, shone and sparkled like jewels. Our ship touched off a recognition flare which was at once replied to by the Admiral. We turned round and steamed slowly ahead of them until a rocket went up as a signal to haul. We then took up station astern of the fleet. Near to us were the lights of two other steamers, which were fish carriers waiting to be loaded up, and far astern were the red and green lights of a sailing ship. The skipper had no doubt the latter belonged to the *Clulow*, and said he would put me on board after breakfast. So I slept for the last time on the hard settee, well content.

I was wakened by the mate shaking me by the shoulder, and though, in the saloon, it was necessary to have the gas lit, I could see the first signs of dawn in the deck prism overhead. 'The *Clulow*'s boat is alongside. They have come for their letters and will take you back with them.'

My three minutes' toilet completed, I went on deck. It was a nasty morning, dark, cold, and lowering, with a strong breeze blowing. As I looked at the madly rising and falling boat alongside, fended off with difficulty by the two men in her, the stuffy, mephitic saloon in the carrier seemed the most desirable home imaginable. But the mate was chucking my dunnage into the boat and I had to follow. It was none too easy to transfer myself from the heavily rolling carrier to the demoniacal boat, but my effort was met with the kindly approval of the *Clulow*'s mate. 'It's easy to see you have been on board a boat before now.' The mate of the carrier was just going to cast off the painter when Bob stopped him. 'You don't mean to tell me they've sent out a doctor and nothing for his dinner!' Thus reminded, the mate dived amongst some ice, produced a joint that looked like a dozen dinners, hove it into the boat and we pushed off. The *Clulow* had worked into a position about half a mile under our lee, and all the boatmen had to do was to let the wind drive us down until we were close under her counter, when a few hard strokes brought us up on her lee side. Watching my chance when the boat was level with the ship's rail, I stepped on board and was warmly greeted by the skipper, a short, heavy, bearded man with a delightful smile. While the crew were getting the boat on board he ordered some breakfast for me and showed me over the ship which was to be my home for several weeks.

The *Clulow* was one of the largest sizes of sailing trawlers converted for Mission purposes. She was one hundred and twenty tons, about ninety feet long and twenty feet broad, and rigged the usual ketch rig. Below decks she had been skilfully adapted for her special duties. Right aft was a small saloon with bunks behind the settees in which the missionaries slept when any were on board. The forrard bulkhead of this compartment had a coal stove between two doors. The starboard door led into my sleeping cabin, which was furnished like any other sleeping cabin, and very comfortable. The port door opened into a long alleyway off which on the port side were a bathroom, storerooms and a well-fitted dispensary; to starboard were the companion and a small hospital with six swinging cots. The forepart of the ship was given up to the crew's quarters and store-rooms in which were stowed the gifts sent by charitable folks to the trawlermen, luxuries such as tobacco and cigarettes, and many little everyday necessities such as men are likely to run out of after several weeks at sea. The crew consisted of eight all told: a skipper, mate, cook, a loblolly boy to assist me, two seamen and two ship's boys. With the exception of the boys and myself they were all deeply religious, and believed they had a direct call from Heaven to the work they were doing in the North Sea. In the midst of much that was evil in the lives of the people around them they were a shining example of the faith that inspired them. They grieved quite openly and frankly over my attitude towards many questions which they believed to be beyond dispute, and only a ruffian could have brought forward any arguments that might have disturbed their simple trust. At the skipper's earnest request I always attended their evening prayers. These chiefly consisted of extempore petitions to the Almighty for a blessing on their work, and a hope that the boys and I might be the subjects of conversion, the whole couched in language that was far from offence, and only betrayed a fervent desire that we would avail ourselves of the blessings granted to them in such abundance.

The routine of the life on board was very simple. Every morning after the haul the trawler-men packed their catch in boxes and sent them off by boat to the carrier. The weather had to be very bad indeed to stop this transfer. After dumping the boxes on the foredeck of the carrier the boat would drop astern along the side of the ship, and this manoeuvre was a constant cause of casualties amongst the boats' crews. If, hampered by the many boats crowding to the carrier, they did not get well clear, the counter of the carrier might, and very often did, come down on top of the boat and smash it to bits. Few of the fishermen could swim; they had a theory that it only prolonged the agony of drowning, and, hampered as they were by oilskins and sea-boots, there was little chance of rescue. The bodies were often brought up in the trawls afterwards. Having got rid of their fish, the men used to make a visit to the *Clulow* to get medical treatment, or to make small purchases. They were a cheery crowd, hard working, and living hard under appalling conditions. Prior to the advent of the Mission ships the fishermen were catered for by an unscrupulous class of ship, usually of Dutch origin, known as 'copers', whose main object was to sell the vilest kinds of spirits at extortionate prices. All governments were agreed that these copers were a menace to the health and morality of the fishermen, but it is only of late years that governments have displayed any desire to interfere in any lucrative trade, however immoral. The real death-blow to this pernicious traffic took place when the Mission supplied a real need by fitting out their ships with reasonable requirements for sale or gift to the fishermen. The *bona fide* purchaser was no longer tempted to make a legitimate shopping expedition the occasion for a drunken orgy. We only saw one of these copers, and a message to the fishery cruiser sent her back to her port at full speed. This traffic no longer exists, as the Mission destroyed it economically, as well as by raising the standard of conduct amongst the men.

As the trawlers spent ten weeks at sea there was plenty of time to run out of many of the little things that make life worth while, and these were supplied by the *Clulow*. As a rule the men were well off and could afford to pay the very moderate prices charged, but if any man was really hard up he was not on that account sent away empty-handed. They all loved coming to the *Clulow*, if only for a yarn and to see fresh faces after being cooped up for weeks in a small ship. On Sundays the men had more time to themselves so, after attending to their mundane requirements, the skipper held a short service, and the lusty shouting of popular hymn tunes by the crews of a dozen trawlers is a thing to remember with delight. The work they did was unbelievably hard, and the only relaxation they ever got was the hour or two they spent on board our ship.

The medical work was very light and chiefly consisted of teeth extractions, purgatives, and the treatment of saltwater boils on their wrists as the result of the hard edge of the oilskin sleeves chafing the flesh when soaked in salt water. Some of these were very bad, but they could be avoided by wearing knitted cuffs which were supplied from the charitable stores.

About that time there was much talk in the press, and especially in the journal called *Truth*, about the cruelty inflicted on apprentices on board the trawlers; and as there were hundreds of trawlers in the North Sea, and all types of men were in command, I have no doubt that there was some truth in the allegations. As far as my own experience went, my belief was that the cruelty was grossly exaggerated for journalistic purposes. Fishermen are not of a bullying or cruel type, and a cheeky, lazy lad can be infernally aggravating. The recognized treatment for this attitude from time immemorial has been a rope's-ending. I came across only one case of bad treatment, and I am sure it was more due to ignorance than to calculated brutality.

An apprentice was sent to me one morning on account of an injury to his right forearm, and I found that one of the bones was broken. I put the arm in splints and would have kept him on board the *Clulow*, the intention being to transfer him by carrier to Guy's Hospital in London, which took all our serious cases. The boy pleaded to be allowed to return to his ship, as she was due to return to his home port at Hull and might leave any day, depending on how her coal lasted. In the circumstances he was sent back, and warned that he must return the next day as there was bound to be some swelling and the bandages would require adjustment. He did not return as ordered, but I hardly expected him, as the sea was very rough, and Bob was unwilling to take me to the trawler, which was a long way to windward of the *Clulow*. On the following day when he did not turn up, although the weather was a little better, I began to feel worried. All kinds of mishaps from gangrene down have happened as the result of swelling under bandages. I had a yarn with Bob and he thought he could make the trawler, so we worked the *Clulow* up to windward of her and got the boat out.

When we got alongside the trawler she was getting her gear up and nobody paid any attention to us or offered to take our line, which was unusual, as the seas were pretty wild and we could have done with some help. Peering over the trawler's bulwarks as the boat danced up and down, I was horrified to see that the boy had his arm out of the sling, and was backing up a warp which was being hove in by the winch. He was lifting the broken arm in his left hand and shifting it along the rope and then hauling, evidently in great pain. This was too much for me and I jumped on the trawler's deck, went up to the boy and angrily demanded what he was doing, and why he had not come to the *Clulow* as ordered. The boy began to cry and said the skipper had set him to work, and had refused to let him come and see me. At this I got very angry indeed and, like all angry men, did what I had no right to do. I seized hold of him and pushed him into our boat, telling Bob to look after him while I went to interview the skipper.

It was rather a job getting the boy into the boat, and when I turned round the skipper was at my elbow demanding with many oaths what I meant by coming between him and his crew. I remonstrated with him on his treatment of the boy, who was really badly injured. His reply was that the boy was an idle young devil, that I was several different kinds of psalm-singing swine, and that he was the man to teach me my place. To wind up with he aimed a blow at my face which would have kept me quiet for a long time if I had not seen it coming and dodged it. He then came at me again, but I was not very much worried as I knew pretty well how to look after myself, or thought I did. When he saw that I did not mean to run away from him he stooped down to remove his seaboots and I flung off my oilskins and did the same. In less than a minute I knew I was in a mess. He knew as much about self-defence as I did and, as he was a much bigger and heavier man, it could be only a question of time before I must go crashing on to the deck. While sparring round, and before I had taken very much punishment, I had a momentary glimpse of Bob's face, full of horrified delight at the scrap, appearing over the edge of the bulwarks, and then the tossing of the boat hid him again. Scared stiff though I was, the sight of that face made me smile, and that suspicion of a smile was the skipper's undoing. He faltered in astonishment, as he knew as well as I did that he had me at his mercy, and, involuntarily, he half turned to see whether I had anything to smile at. That gave me my chance and I caught him a whopper on the point. He went over on the wooden forehatch which formed the ring, hit his head a nasty whack and lay still. For a moment I thought he was seriously injured, and had a horrid vision of being tried for manslaughter on the high seas. But he picked himself up and made no further attempt to strike me. Muttering, 'You can keep the bloody boy if you want to', he strode aft and disappeared below. The crew of the trawler had stood sulkily round during the fracas, but made no effort at interfering with me as I hung on the rail waiting for a chance to get into my boat.

As we pulled back to the *Clulow* Bob's eyes were dancing, though his tongue reproved me for the sins of hasty temper, brawling, and unjustifiable interference with a master on board his own vessel. The boy was transferred to another trawler leaving for Hull, and he was grateful enough for my interference to say that I had got him into a nice row with his skipper. Bob related my misdeeds to the skipper of the *Clulow* with a wealth of detail and a keen appreciation of the nicer points of the scrap, punctuated by much doleful shaking of the head. The impression left on my own mind was that he had not enjoyed himself so much for many a long day, and later I got him to confess that in his unregenerate days he had been a well-known boxer.

We had no missionaries on board during the time I was at sea, and it was just as well since, if they had not been immune to seasickness, they would have been a nuisance to themselves and everybody else on the ship. I had the saloon to myself and it was a cosy spot. The carriers brought papers and letters regularly and I had plenty of books, so that the time passed astonishingly quickly, and I found it difficult to believe in the blessings of the land. The weather of the last two months of the year is notoriously bad, and as there was no shelter to run for we had to see it out where we were. There were several gales, but we rode them out, hove-to, in perfect comfort, and it is a tribute to the seaworthiness of these vessels that there was never any anxiety as far as the sea alone was concerned.

One afternoon I watched a heavily laden timber steamer, with a preposterous deck cargo, which was battling with the fury of a north-east gale. She was a mile or so to windward of us and seemed to be making little or no headway. Every now and then the force of the wind on her huge superstructure pushed her broadside on to the wind and sea, and then we could see the waves making a complete breach over her. Bob, who was keeping watch on deck, said that her condition was desperate, and he wondered what was going to happen to her if the gale did not let up. In a specially fierce squall she got broadside on, and although they must have made frantic efforts to bring her head to wind the pressure of the wind was so great that, after listing heavily for a short time, she finally lay down on her side and slowly sank. Her deck load was already scattered all over the sea to leeward of her, and through the glasses I could see the heads of men clinging to the balks of timber. We were hove to at the time and, not thinking what I was doing, I sprang to the wheel and started casting the lashings adrift, at the same time shouting to Bob to let the staysail draw. Instead of doing what I expected, Bob came flying aft to the wheel, tore it out of my hands and put the helm up so as to run away from the wreckage. 'What are you doing?' I yelled at him as I fought to regain possession of the wheel. 'There are men drowning over there.' His expression convinced me more than his arguments. 'God help them! They'll have to drown! Any one of them balks would be through our sides long before we got anywhere near them.' Even while we argued, proof of the truth of his statement was being borne down upon us by the strength of the gale, and it was only with the utmost difficulty we managed to save our own ship. But for years after I woke up at night telling myself I was a coward and had left helpless men to drown.

In fine light weather the Admiral told off a trawler to tow us to the next fishing ground, but when it was blowing hard we were, perforce, left to ourselves, a shouted message as to the rendezvous being given or, if that were impossible, we followed the example of the carrier and asked our way. The result was that we were often separated from our own particular fleet for days, but we fell in with others, and rendered any help we were asked for or gave any stores that might be wanted. The North Sea fishermen have an intimate knowledge of the bottom of the area in which they work, and their charts are as full of names as a map of London streets, while they know the nature of the ground as well as one knows the features of one's home town. In all the hollows fish are to be caught, and the Admiral has an uncanny insight into the habits and migration of the fish, and follows them with unerring instinct. If he does not, the result will be reflected in the catches of the fleet under him, and the owners will soon replace him by a more capable man, while the erstwhile Admiral becomes the mere skipper of a trawler again. The appointment of Admiral was a most lucrative one, since, in addition to his pay and share as the skipper of a trawler, he got a share in the whole catch of the fleet under his control. Some of these Admirals were said to make over a thousand a year.

Their methods of navigation were simple, and entirely the fruits of experience. When in doubt as to their position they took a cast of the lead, considered the depth, looked at the arming carefully, smelt it and then rubbed their tongue over it. The latter process gave them an idea of the coarseness of the bottom sand, and was the only way they could gauge it as their hands were not sensitive enough. After a little thought they would give the position to within a mile or so, and there was rarely any error in the statement. I only once found our skipper in a difficulty. Coming on deck at midday I noticed he had a sextant in his hand, and was looking very worried. As I had never seen him use the instrument before, and did not even know there was one on board, I asked what the trouble was. He explained that he was doubtful as to his exact whereabouts as there were places, north and south of the Dogger where the depths and bottom were so much alike that it was impossible to distinguish between them by the lead alone. We were over one of these patches now and he had hoped to be able to say which with the help of a meridian altitude. He had just taken one and worked it out, but the result had placed somewhere in the middle of France, which, as dear old Euclid used to say, was absurd. Thinking there might be an error in the sextant, he had brought it on deck again to see if there was, but it seemed to be all right, and he was completely puzzled. I made a hasty calculation that seemed to show that his altitude was not far out, and suggested that he must have made a mistake in working the problem. I overhauled his figures, and was able to show him that he had made an error in applying his declination. After working it out properly, I was able to assure him that, if the distance between the patches was as great as he said, we must be over the northern one.

Later soundings showed that this was right, but the skipper never ceased to wonder that a doctor could take an interest in navigation. The only one he had ever met who knew anything about the subject was Wilfred Grenfell, and thereafter I heard much about my famous predecessor. Shortly before this he had gone out to his life's work in Labrador, and it is no exaggeration to say that he was worshipped by everyone, irrespective of creed or want of it, with whom he had come in contact. The simple manliness of Grenfell had influenced for good thousands who would have been deaf to the appeals of the ordinary missionary.

It was time for the ship to go back to Yarmouth to refit and to give leave to the crew after their ten weeks at sea. One morning we sailed down the whole length of the fleet, and I heard for the last time the cheery North Sea hail, 'How many boxes last night?' A couple of days of drift in light winds brought us to the Corton lightship in an early morning fog, and when that cleared a tug picked us up and towed the ship up river to her wharf. A hasty interview with the Mission officials, a visit to the barber to remove a gingery beard, and by 10 p.m. I was on board a steamer bound to Hull and Leith. I did not join the ship again as time did not permit, but until after the war I kept as one of my most cherished possessions a model of the *Clulow* carved and rigged by the skilful hands of old Bob.

III

'Dorothy'

SHE WAS OLD AND UNUTTERABLY DISREPUTABLE when I had my first sight of her lying on the beach at Penrhyn. I cursed my pathetic trust in the advertisement, 'Sound and seaworthy cruiser for sale', that had brought me all the way from Chatham at a cost of over five pounds. Varnish did not exist, paint had blistered off in huge flakes everywhere, her bottom planking was bare, and rust and neglect were rapidly hastening her towards dissolution. It was hardly worth going any farther, I thought, but 'Better have a look at her now that you have come so far' was suggested by the caretaker in reply to my snort of disappointment. 'You haven't taken much care of her. What do you think you were paid for?' 'I wasn't paid for doing anything, and that's what's the matter with her. She's perfectly sound and good whatever she looks like. I'm a poor man and I can't afford to keep up other people's boats out of my own pocket.' This argument was unanswerable, and I climbed on board fretting and fuming, my wrath transferred to the owner who had written such glowing descriptions of the beauty of his ship.

Down below there was the same evidence of neglect, but the accommodation was unusually good for a 13-ton yawl, and I was soon able to assure myself that there was nothing a little labour and cleanliness could not put to rights. Then I went over the side and, armed with a hammer and knife which I used freely, made a preliminary survey as to her condition. Whilst I worked my companion shed what light he could on her history. She was built by Musselwhite in Poole about twenty-five years before as a pilot boat, and after some years of service had been converted into a yacht by building a coach roof over the well. The ship was not registered, and did not appear in any yacht list, so it was impossible to confirm or deny his statements but, as I proceeded with my examination, I had ample proof that she had been well and faithfully built by a master craftsman. There was nothing the matter with the outside planking, so the survey of the frames was undertaken as far as was possible. The scrap-iron ballast was cemented in, and it was out of the question to be able to say what was happening under the cement, but as the frames were perfectly sound where they disappeared under the cement, I was of opinion that they must be all right.

Her dimensions proved to be: length, thirty-three feet; waterline, thirty feet; beam, ten feet; draught, five feet. It was the draught that had originally appealed to me when I read the advertisement, as I had longings to visit the Dutch canals, and everything I knew about these fascinating waterways pointed to five feet as the maximum draught permissible if one wanted to see much of the country.

The result of my examination was so satisfactory that I got an estimate from the caretaker for hogging her out, cleaning off all the old paint and varnish, outside and inside, and repainting and revarnishing to my specification. Having subtracted this sum from the price quoted to me I made an offer which was so promptly accepted that it left me wondering whether I had been unduly generous. In reply to my remarks on the state the ship was in, the owner, who lived in the north of England, said that he had been shamefully served by the people he had entrusted with her care. That ought to have opened my eyes, but at the time I put it down to the spleen of a man who had found out that property deteriorates unless you spend money on its upkeep.

There are no official formalities about the transfer of an unregistered vessel to a new owner. I sent a cheque for which I received a receipt and the ship was mine. There was something humiliating about the whole transaction, as I felt it had not taken place with the law-inspired solemnity that the importance of the occasion demanded. The absence of the familiar carving on the main-beam giving the ship's official number and her registered tonnage, the fact that I had no beautifully engrossed parchment proclaiming to all and sundry that I was the sole owner of sixty-four sixty-fourths of the above-named vessel along with her arms and accoutrements, the knowledge that I was too unimportant to have appended my signature to a bill of sale or attested in front of reputable witnesses that I was a free-born British subject and, as such, entitled to be the owner of the said vessel, and to proceed to sea on my lawful occasions—all these disadvantages were poorly compensated for by the assurance of the caretaker that I need not pay any light dues. Gladly would I have paid the Custom House the paltry sum of four shillings and sixpence annually, which I calculated was the amount I owed Trinity House for the lighthouses, lightships and buoys so plentifully strewn about the coast to help me in my need. I felt I could not look a lightship in the face without it knowing me for the bilker I was. So I set to work to remedy this state of affairs and to join the magic circle of those who were entitled to fly the blue or defaced ensign—whichever the club I belonged to was entitled to wear.

Anyone who has ever tried to register an ancient vessel which has passed through the hands of many owners can easily guess what happened. Officialdom would have nothing to do with me or my four and sixpence, and refused me the longed-for passport into approved yachting society unless I could work miracles and fulfil absolutely impossible conditions, one of the least of which was to produce receipts from the previous owners showing that her sale had been a legitimate transaction. Finally, after six months of unremitting effort, I gave it up, and am glad to say that none of the pains and penalties supposed to be attached to the ownership of an unregistered vessel ever materialized. In foreign waters my painfully respectable appearance must have been a guarantee of my good faith, since at no time was my ownership challenged. But at home I shrank into myself when an unfeeling brute of a Customs officer or a grasping harbour master demanded in raucous tones, 'What is your net registered tonnage?' I always answered with hate in my heart, 'Ten tons'. It was a nice easy number to remember, and was so obviously not an understatement that I was little likely to be asked to produce my registration certificate to prove it. But, except in the eyes of the courteous, I was not a yacht. I suppose I had joined the class so well described by a beautiful young thing on Cowes green whom I heard explaining the mysteries to a still more vivid friend. 'I always know a yacht when I see one.' 'My! Aren't you wonderful! How in all the world can you tell them?' 'It's quite easy, really, when you know. When they've got a funnel that's a yacht.' The friend's eyes wandered over the yachts of every size, shape, and rig which only Cowes can show on a summer afternoon, and funnels were few and far between. Doubt seemed to creep into her mind and she enquired. 'Then what are all the others?' 'Those?' The lady sniffed as contemptuously as the hard-case captain of a full-rigged ship. 'Those are just motor-boats.'

While *Dorothy* was being fitted out at Falmouth I was in thrall at Chatham, but dreaming all the time of how much had been accomplished by the army of workmen who, I imagined, got up in the morning feeling that the world was a purer and better place for the work they had done yesterday, but nothing to what it would be when they had finished the toil of to-day. The weather was bad at the time, and my heart went out to these stalwart and skilful British artisans enduring such backbreaking toil under adverse conditions just for my pleasure. But then I thought what a stupid way of looking at it—think rather of these fine fellows enjoying the work of their hands and, as they look at the gleaming hull, how they say to themselves, 'It is good'.

I knew there was an army of men working on my behalf because the answer to my letter to the caretaker, telling him that the purchase had been completed, and that he could get on with the fitting out at the agreed estimate, asked for a look at the receipt. I thought this rather unusual, but I had little experience in buying yachts, and I was still a little under the weather over the registration business, and came to the conclusion that he was justified in protecting himself against any attempt at fraud, so I sent the receipt which was duly returned. The covering letter stated that the writer was a poor man and it was necessary to employ men, number unspecified, in order to complete the work by the time I had suggested. In short he wanted an advance 'on account'. As the amount he asked for was very nearly the whole sum agreed upon for the job, I felt half ashamed of myself that I had been so harsh in my bargaining with the honest fellow, since—only to please me, mark you!—he was evidently going to spend most of the money on outside labour, leaving very little for himself. I was so touched with this disinterested action that I sent the cheque, and promised that if the work were done to my satisfaction I would pay him a bonus of ten pounds in addition to the sum we had agreed upon. His acknowledgment only too clearly indicated the trials his sense of duty towards me was causing him to undergo, and there were many references to the terrible weather they had to face in Falmouth. The bonus was not really required to spur him on to do his duty, but he welcomed the promise of it as showing that I possessed the right spirit. I wanted to run down to Falmouth after this letter just to see how the work was getting on, and give him the words of encouragement and understanding that he hinted his soul longed for; but the Admiralty had an absurdly mistaken belief in my importance in their scheme of things, and it was impossible to get away from Chatham without encroaching on my long leave. Every day of this must be jealously preserved for the great cruise which was approaching on leaden feet.

A fortnight before I was due to join I received a request that my hand should be sent down to Falmouth to be put in touch with the rigging of the ship. My reply was that I intended to sail the ship single-handed, and that when rigging her this was to be borne in mind, and every effort made to make the work as easy as possible. The answer was that the yacht had never been sailed single-handed before, that she was not meant for single-handed work, that some help was absolutely necessary as the weather had been so bad that they were behindhand with the work, and that if I had no hand in prospect the writer could recommend a very good one at twenty-five shillings a week with everything found. I refused this offer, and gave an arbitrary order, in my best naval manner, that the ship was to be ready at the agreed time or no further payments would be made. There was no reply to this and I thought I had 'larned him'.

The long-looked-for day at length arrived, and after somewhat rashly assuring my senior officer that I would comply with the Admiralty regulations and keep in touch with the department by telegraph, I was free to do what I willed for six weeks. The visions that passed through my mind as the train crawled its weary way to Falmouth could only have been adequately represented by a marine artist of the highest ability. It was a sodden, beastly day, but I could see nothing except sunlight playing on snowy canvas, and a gleaming hull beneath. On arrival at Falmouth conditions had not improved, and the figure of the caretaker, who met me at the station, was clad in streaming oilskins. In response to my eager enquiries about the ship he waved his arm around and damped my spirits as well as my hat by groaning: 'What can a man do in weather like this? We've had nothing else since you were down here last.'

I knew that Falmouth had a well-earned reputation for being wetter than most places in the British Isles, but it was difficult to believe that there had been more than thirty-one without a single gleam of sun as the old rhyme has it, but the weather had been sufficiently bad in the east country to make it likely that it had been worse here. 'Well, I suppose the paint work will be all right anyhow,' I said, referring to his promise that this would be done under cover. A noncommittal silence was evidently meant to prepare me for disappointment.

A smelly, depressed-looking growler, with a horse and driver both in the last stages of senile decay, carried us down to the quay where the dinghy was lying. I could swear that the old horse, as soon as it heard our destination, muttered 'Yachtsman!' and took no further interest in the proceedings, but I could have wrung the driver's neck when he grinned offensively and said something about fine yachting weather. He was still grinning as if he had some inward joke when I had paid the amount he grossly overcharged me.

The dinghy was my first shock. It was obviously in the same condition as when I had seen it last in the store, and it was completely bare of varnish, and had not even been washed down. When I expressed my surprise that nothing had been done to it, I received the reply that that work had not been included in the estimate. My business arrangements have always been bad, and the whole of our agreement was a verbal one, and though I remembered mentioning the dinghy when we were discussing the work to be done it was possible that a genuine mistake had been made. I then asked why he had not mentioned the dinghy in his letters as he must have known that I wanted it done up. His reply was, 'I did mention it but you took no notice.' This was a barefaced lie, and he knew it was as well as I did, so the rest of the passage was made in resentful silence.

I had had my dreams and the less said about the realization the better. In ever-increasing wrath and bitterness I surveyed the work that had been done. Apart from putting the gear on board it was impossible to believe that anything had been done to the ship at all. Even the bilges had not been cleaned out, and the whole ship was sodden, stinking, and filthy. There was a row, of course, but I was helpless in the hands of a master rascal. The final insult added to much injury was when he demanded the bonus of ten pounds because the work had been satisfactorily done.

I refused to pay this last extortion, and as I pulled him ashore in the disreputable dinghy he told me he was off to take a summons out against me. This would have meant interminable delay, and when the case was heard it would have been a question of hard swearing, his word against mine. Sick and disgusted with the whole affair I gave in and paid up. I have never been able to raise any great enthusiasm for Falmouth since this affair.

Back on board to spend the most miserable evening I have ever experienced. Luckily I had brought some blankets with me, and they were the only dry articles in the ship. The cooking stove in the fo'c'sle was a Rippingille in gimbals, but the paraffin reservoirs were full of a mixture of oil and water, and refused to function until they had been emptied and the wicks cleaned. It took longer to find out what was the trouble than to remedy it, and once it was going in the saloon with a primus (a new toy in those days) which I had brought with me, there was an overpowering odour of mildew and fetid steam that drove me gasping to endure the rain in the cockpit.

After a cup of tea and a boiled egg I began a little ruefully to see the funny side of the business, and realized just how big a fool I had been from the very beginning. I had, probably for the first time in yachting history, agreed to pay the price asked by a seller instead of following the usual custom of making a firm offer. Why yachtsmen should have a monopoly of firm offers, and all other merchants deal in wobbly ones, I cannot imagine. Not so long ago Cornwall was a nation of wreckers, and the inhabitants of one township still looked on

My single-handed cruiser

interlopers even from a nearby town as foreigners and natural enemies. I had heard of a postman who had married a girl from a neighbouring village, who had been cut by the whole of his native village because he had married a foreigner. My friend, the caretaker, was a local preacher of the militant type, and he was fluently acquainted with all the imprecations in the Old Testament. He had learned from the receipt which I had been foolish enough to send him exactly the kind of blithering idiot that had been delivered into his hands. Fortified by the knowledge that a fool and his money are soon parted, he was out in perfectly good faith to spoil the Egyptians, lay waste the Philistines, and smite the Amalekites hip and thigh. I hope that I have got these quotations right or, even in the specially designed Gehenna he at present inhabits, I can see a sneer on his ugly mug as he learns the depth of my ignorance of the things that really matter.

To counterbalance the loss of my money which, thanks to a lack of adequate appreciation of the value of my services by a misguided Admiralty, I could ill afford to lose, I began to count my blessings in accordance with the precepts of my old nurse. I have always claimed that all the spice of life lay in its vivid contrasts, the more decided so much the more soul-satisfying. A dinner at the Café Royal one night followed by a sausage and mash at a low eating-house in the Strand the next; a luxury hotel for one day's lodging (I could rarely afford a longer stay), alternating with a spell of bug-ridden lodgings; a reception at the Commander-in-Chief's, succeeded by the privilege of a platform seat to listen to, and apparently by my presence approve of, one of Jim Larkin's rhodomantades; a seawise passage in the first-class cabin of a P & O liner, and the same trip in the 'excellent loneliness' of a single-handed five-ton cutter. These were a few of the experiences that filled my soul with satisfaction, and made me feel that it was good to be alive. The difference between my dream in the train and my real surroundings provided another sop to my longing for change as a refuge from monotonous routine. Also I discovered that one very real hardship was absent in my present plight. As far as I could make out the ship did not leak anywhere either above or below decks. That was an improvement on my first little ship, *Orion*, where I had to sleep on the cabin floor between the settees in bad weather, and I knew when my back got wet it was time to get up and pump if I wanted to keep the ship afloat. Nor were there going to be any drips on my sleeping face, which was better luck than I had in one of Her Majesty's ships, where I used to sleep with an oilskin draped over my bunk, and an extended umbrella over my head to prevent the condensation drips from disturbing my slumbers.

By putting out the stoves the atmosphere became bearable, so I rolled myself in the dry blankets, pillowed my head on a malodorous cushion, listened appreciatively to the patter of the rain on the deck overhead, and slept the sleep of the amateur cruiser. Need I say more?

When I woke up at six o'clock next morning Falmouth was begging to be forgiven. The sun was shining, not too brilliantly, and the cackle of the little waves driven by the south-west wind against the bows was a sheer joy to hear in its suggestion of beckoning music. The level rays of the rising sun which had wakened me up by playing on my eyelids streamed into the cabin through the scuttles, and converted that dingy smelly kennel into the home of true romance. I jumped up and lit the stove, then pushed open the slide and, with deep breaths, tried to absorb and make mine for ever the beauty of the morning. There was no *Cutty Sark*, that dreary museum piece with its pathetic suggestion of the death of sail, but everywhere I looked there were the masts and yards of the little topsail schooners, barquentines, and ketches that were still bravely defying their inevitable defeat by steam, and the clank, clank of their windlasses showed that some of them were bound to the eastward and were anxious not to waste a fair wind. Out in the Carrick roads were the tall masts of half a dozen four-posters calling at Falmouth for orders. The phrase meant something in those days. All over the harbour and reaching out into the roads were endless quay punts going about their business on the waters, heedless of the fast approaching day when they were to be hawked about by their bankrupt owners as desirable yachts. Over towards St. Mawes a Falmouth pilot boat was working her way out to her station, which might be anywhere up to ten degrees west. These too are gone, but in those days there was no need for a *Cutty Sark* to tear the heart of the sailorman with vague yearnings for the glorious past of sail. To me, no prophet, it was only Falmouth harbour. But, as long as I live, my mind at the keen caress of a breeze and the whiff of a tarry rope will subconsciously evoke that unforgettable scene in all its splendid detail.

My annoyance at my treatment of yesterday had completely gone, and I only remembered it a bit ruefully as became the victim of a not very kindly practical joke. I had learned in the Service how to carry off my chagrin at that kind of treatment. I had my boat, her hull was sound and good, and I had six weeks in front of me in which to sail her back to Chatham. Long before we arrived there I would have her, if not the shining beauty of my dreams, at least good to look at. But I was not going to give amusement to that psalm-singing humbug by letting him see me do the work for which I had so outrageously paid him. The first thing to do was to get away from Falmouth, and after a wash-down—and didn't she want it, poor dear?—and a comfortable breakfast I weighed the kedge. After shortening in on the main anchor I got off the sail-covers, hoisted the mainsail, set the head-sails in stops and rove off the sheets. Then, after making sure that I had a clear passage in the direction I wanted to go, I finished all the other jobs and got under way. It sounds simple, but, new to the gear as I was, it took me three hours of hard work before I was able to bear away and run out of the harbour on the starboard jibe.

I had never handled a yacht of this size by myself before, and I was rapidly being taught a great deal I had no overpowering desire to learn. The previous owner had always carried two hands, and two hands on board a ship the size of this one have to do something to justify their existence, or even the most ignorant of owners will very soon come to the conclusion that his wages bill is out of all proportion to the work that is being done, and reduce his staff accordingly. So these two men had set to work to make their numbers indispensable, and their method of arranging the lead of the head sheets so that it was necessary to have two men to get them in properly compelled my reluctant admiration, and much hard swearing. Something would have to be done about it when I got to Fowey— if I ever got there, about which I was doubtful if the wind headed me. I chuckled as I imagined an ignominious return to Falmouth and the jeers of the tub-thumper at my refusal to employ his friend as a hand. But with Helford River under my lee, in case of a shift of wind, I felt fairly safe from being compelled to endure that last debacle.

Nothing untoward happened. The wind fell lighter and lighter, and I drifted into Fowey late in the afternoon, and anchored close under Polruan so as to be clear of any incoming swell. It was as well I did, for that night it blew a strong south-west gale, and I was rolled out of my bunk several times. My usual refuge on these occasions, the floor, was so wide that I kept colliding violently with the legs of the table or the side of the settees. Morning saw some diminution of the strength of the gale, but a nasty sea was running into Readymoney cove, and a big ketch yacht lying in the main channel of the harbour was rolling her gunwale under. I suppose one ought to have foreseen this gale, but the glass had given no warning of its approach, and there were no weather forecasts to keep us tucked away in snug harbours. Weather forecasting by a single observer is a chancy business at the best of times, and this is well illustrated by a conversation I once held with an old fisherman on St. Mawes pier. In reply to my question what he thought about the weather he pondered long and deeply, and spat quite a lot before he delivered himself of this oracular utterance. 'I don't know what to think about it. I'd like to see the wind come in a bit... The glass is steady.' And that is as far as most of us got. So we just sailed when the tide suited and took what was coming to us with such philosophy as we could muster. I do not think we were any the worse sailors or were less carefully fitted out for this outlook.

In spite of the shelter of Polruan *Dorothy* rolled and rolled and rolled. Work of any kind was an impossibility, and I spent most of the morning searching for some loose article which rolled backwards and forwards with maddening persistency, and nearly drove me crazy with annoyance at my failure to find it. Several times I thought I had done so only to be disillusioned a few minutes later by the recurrence of the irritating little noise. The big ketch rigged storm canvas, clad her crew in oilskins and, with the aid of a tug, put out to sea evidently under the impression that they could not be more uncomfortable there than in harbour. I fully agreed with them, and made up my mind to follow at the first opportunity. Nowadays we would get our anchor, switch on our engine, and steam up to the peace and comfort of the anchorage called the Wiseman's Stone. At that time few yachting visitors to Fowey knew of this anchorage, since it required power to reach it on account of baffling flaws on the passage.

Later in the afternoon I decided I could not stand the discomfort of the rolling any longer and, although it was still blowing hard, I got the ship under way under very short canvas and stood away for the entrance. Although I had done my best to improve the lead of the head sheets I was unable to get the ship round when close to the rocks on the western side of the harbour. There was some excuse for her, poor old thing, as there was a heavy tumbling sea with backwash from the rocks, while the wind was nothing but a series of shifting squalls. There was nothing for it but to up helm, slack away the main sheet, and wear her round so as to get into an advantageous position for another try. That too was a failure, and for a moment I thought I had lost her when a breaking sea threw me towards the rocks whilst I was in the act of wearing round again. I made a third effort, impelled by the recollection of the rolling misery of the anchorage, but I realized this time that I had not sufficient canvas set to keep her going in the calm patches that alternated with the heavy squalls, so I reluctantly went back to Polruan and dropped the killick*. I had been toiling strenuously for four hours and was exhausted. My first attempt at sailing her single-handed in strong weather had not been a conspicuous success.

My efforts had been a source of intense interest to some stormbound Polruan fishermen, and after I had got things squared up two of them came off in their boat to remonstrate with me for attempting to put to sea on such a day, and especially in a boat like mine. Now I had been her owner long enough to have reached that state once described by a yachting friend as the one when the pride of possession is so great that you would sooner tolerate a slur on the wife of your bosom than a reflection on the ship of your dreams, of which you

---

*   A small anchor or 'lunch hook'. —Ed

felt yourself 'absolute master and dominant lord', so I asked a bit tartly what they knew about it. It turned out that they knew or claimed to know quite a lot. Her draught was wrong for turning to windward in a seaway, her sail plan was wrong, her hull was wrong, her leads were wrong, and they left me in little doubt, although they did not actually say so, that I was the most wrong-headed part of the whole contraption in imagining that I could sail her without assistance. Experience, as well as my aching limbs and barked knuckles, seemed to prove that in this latter assumption they were probably right, so I meekly thanked them for their advice, and asked whether they could recommend a good hand. Here I drew a blank as all the yachting hands were already engaged and away in their ships. It was too late in the season to find a good man unemployed. With that curious perversity I have often noticed amongst fishermen, they claimed to be able to supply me with the names and addresses of plenty of dirty rascals for whom hanging was too good a fate, and left me wondering whether they considered, in view of my recent exhibition of seamanship, that sailing with me might not be an excellent and easy way of ridding Polruan of some unwanted and undesirable residents. I refused to contribute to the welfare of the community in this self-sacrificing fashion but, as they shoved off, one of them suggested that I might find a hand off one of the coasting schooners in the Sailors' Home where they stayed when they were out of a job. This is how I found Vincent. But he deserves a chapter to himself.

IV

Vincent

AFTER ANOTHER EXASPERATING NIGHT of rolling, although the gale had taken
off a bit and the wind still refused to come in, I went across to Fowey. I
found the Sailors' Home easily enough and stated my quest for a yacht hand
to the wife of the caretaker who answered my ring. She shook her head de-
spondently and, eyeing my really rather smart yachting rig, which John Gieve
had kindly put down to my account when I explained that I must have something to 'go' with my dream ship, said she was sure there was no suitable person in the Home; in fact there was only one man resident and he would not
do at all. I asked whether I might be allowed to have a look at him as my need
was urgent and she, doubtingly, led me to the common room where, at eleven
in the forenoon, a man was sitting at a bare deal table apparently deliberating
whether he was able to tackle the appetizing breakfast spread temptingly in
front of him. He did not turn round as we entered, and all I could see was a
huge shock of fiery red hair and a powerful looking back. The woman left us,
and I sat down on the form on the opposite side of the table, a movement to
which he did not pay the slightest attention. I learned afterwards that he had
not meant to be discourteous, but imagined that I was one of the junior officers from one of the china clay steamers who had come into the Home for a
meal. I came to grips at once.

'I am sorry to disturb you whilst you are having your breakfast.'

'I ain't having no breakfast.' He really meant that he was at my service and
that I need not feel embarrassed, though, in my ignorance, I translated his
sentiments differently.

His face was small, and he had tiny china-blue eyes with red rims
fringed with long, bright-red eyelashes. Bushy red eyebrows projected from

his forehead like an outcrop of red sandstone in a field of wheat. A stubbly red scrub all over his face was the fruit of his conviction that, in unaccustomed hands, the old-fashioned cut-throat razor was a dangerous weapon, and as such to be avoided by a man of good sense. He never got over his belief that my habit of shaving every morning was a needless addition to the perils of the sea.

In the meantime he blinked owlishly at me across the table and waited for me to continue.

'I am looking for a hand for my yacht. Would you like to take the job on?'

This took some thinking over. He looked at the golden badge on my snowy-crowned yachting cap, shifted his scrutiny to my double-breasted blue jacket, and then let fall these words of wisdom:

'Stooard's buttons.'

In accordance with the custom of my tribe the club buttons on my jacket were made of horn, brass buttons being left to professional crews in order to distinguish the owner from his hirelings by the modesty of his apparel. On board merchant ships the steward branch often wear black horn buttons, so I knew what was on his mind and hastened to reassure him.

'I'm the owner all right. It's not a steward I am looking for but a seaman.' I grinned in a friendly manner at his mistake. He brightened up.

'What wages were you offering?'

'Wait a bit my friend. I'm not offering anything until I know a little more about you. Can you hand, reef and steer?'

'Eh?'

'Do you know your job as a seaman?'

'I bin one afore you were born.'

'Why did you leave your last ship?'

'I never left her. She left me. When I woke up she was gone.' He struggled to suppress an overwhelming sense of having been unjustly treated.

'What was she?'

'A tawpsail schooner out of Bideford. And that skipper owes me three months' money, and he'll say I forfeited the money by deserting.' Clouds of frothy spume were blowing from his mouth and soaking his disreputable moustache.

'That was why he left you, I expect, to get out of paying you your money.'

'You've guessed right this time.' He sank back into a malevolent reverie.

'Well, I am offering you twenty-five shillings a week and all found.'

'But I got two pun ten a month in the schooner and everything found.' He glared wrathfully at my mean effort at sweating a broken man.

'When you managed to get it,' I said. 'Don't be an idiot. I am offering you five pounds a month and everything found.'

'I'll come.'

'Better see the ship first and hear about the job before you make up your mind.'

'I'll come all right.'

But I refused to allow him to consider himself engaged until he had seen what he was letting himself in for. I did not know much about the living and working conditions in the foc's'le of a coasting schooner, and I was afraid that he would find his quarters on board a small yacht distinctly cramped, and that the lack of companionship would be a great privation. He took very little interest in the inspection. For him it was only another job. The four-feet-nine headroom in the foc's'le worried him not at all as he was only five feet high, and he habitually moved about on his spindly little legs as if he expected a swinging block overhead to catch him a clout. Finally, we sat down in the saloon and I asked him what he thought about it. The only interest he had betrayed was when he picked up the manrope knot on the gangway stanchions, and after a moment's scornful scrutiny dropped it as if it hurt. That same knot had been painfully evolved by myself as a tribute to the gleaming beauty of my dreams.

'I'll come,' he said, eyeing with disfavour the appointments of the saloon.

'Are you anything of a cook?'

'I ain't no stooard, sir.'

His eye was watery so my next question was made with some diffidence.

'Do you drink at all?'

'I ain't no teetotaller and I ain't no drunkard.'

Later I was to find that he had been absurdly modest in his estimate of his abilities in both these spheres of activity. He was quite a passable cook and, when it came to drinking, well—that will be seen later.

He had no money, whether due to his own delinquencies or the action of his late skipper, so I gave him an advance of a week's wages to settle his bill at the Home and to buy some gear so that, as he put it, he could come 'respectable'. I put him ashore after he had faithfully promised to be on board by eight o'clock next morning as my intention was to sail at ten. During the night I began to wonder if I would ever see Vincent again, and this doubt seemed justified the following morning when eight, nine, and ten passed and he did not appear. I had just been debating how many ports in Cornwall were going to make me feel the perfect ass when he hove in sight, rowed by a local waterman. From the language they were using to one another they were not, apparently, on the best of terms. 'I did,' and 'You didn't,' followed by, 'I tell you I did,' and 'I tell you you didn't,' were being shouted at the tops of their voices, and now and then the rower stopped rowing to shake his fist under the nose of Vincent, who returned the gesticulation with added vigour. As they came alongside there was a final exchange of 'dids' and 'didn'ts', a valedictory chorus of threats accompanied by violent brandishing of arms and fists, and Vincent, with his baggage, had arrived.

On my angry request for an explanation of his delay he told a long-winded story of how he had arranged with, and paid, the boatman the night before, but on coming down to the jetty in plenty of time the fellow was not to be found, and he had only turned up five minutes ago. I asked why he had not got hold of another boatman, but he said he had no money left as he had spent it all, and none of the boatmen would believe him when he said that he was a hand on board a yacht. As I had a sneaking sympathy with the unbelievers I had to admit that there was a certain amount of plausibility in his excuse and accept it. But the oral honours of the day remained with the boatman, who had held on alongside to listen to our argument. As he pushed off he cast a withering look at me and shouted as he receded: 'If you follow where that

head leads you you'll come to a place where its colour will never be noticed.'
Experience has taught me that Vincent had the perfect answer ready, but respect for his new employer sadly hampered his style. He contented himself
with pointedly turning his back on his enemy and suggestively rubbing a certain portion of his anatomy. The boatman must have been an expert in the
translation of sign language since this action reduced him to a state of foaming
hysteria. Pleased with the success of his tactics, Vincent turned to me with a
childish grin, but when I asked him whether the boatman was a local preacher
the grin was replaced by a vacant stare, and I had to remember that I was a
Scot and only joked with difficulty.

In ten minutes his gear was stowed below and, dressed in a ragged old
Guernsey and a disreputable pair of tweed trousers, Vincent came on deck
and began work. He was a revelation. Without looking at what he was doing or
taking the least care of any kind he seemed to know by intuition where every
block and rope in the ship were placed and what were their uses. He never put
his hand on the wrong thing or looked aloft to see the lead of the ropes, and
he only faltered once when he came to the leads of the head sheets. 'Making
work, I call it,' he shouted aft to me. 'We'll have to change all this before we
go to sea again.' He was a figure of fun on shore, but on board a sailing ship
he was a man in a man's place. Though there was little improvement in the
weather, and the seas were still awkward, we beat out of the narrow entrance
of Fowey harbour like a bird, and a little later, when we had made sufficient
offing, were scudding before a strong wind and a heavy sea.

Vincent had not asked where we were going or anything about our ultimate destination; the matter did not seem to have the slightest interest for
him, but I told him we were going to the Yealm. If I had told him we were
bound for Timbuctoo I am convinced that he would not have shown any more
concern even if he had known where Timbuctoo was. The wind and sea increased as we lost what little shelter the Dodman had hitherto afforded us,
and he approached me to ask how far it was to this 'ere Yealm. I said about
twenty miles, and then he expressed the opinion that we could carry on for
that distance without taking in another reef. I agreed, and we settled down for

our four hours' run. I am a moderately good helmsman, but running hard in a heavy sea steering a short beamy boat is tiring work, and there was just that much danger in it that I was unwilling to entrust it to an unaccustomed hand. After a couple of hours of it I had reached that stage when I would have given a lot for a spell and a smoke. At that moment Vincent sidled up astern of me in the cockpit and placed his hand on the straining tiller. 'You go below and have a smoke, sir, I'll take her for a bit.' Doubtfully I let him take the strain and watched how he shaped, ready to take charge in an instant if anything went wrong. And then I rose with a sigh and went below. That man was my master, and compared with him I was branded amateur all over.

As we approached the tricky entrance to the Yealm I tried to get him to take an interest in the pilotage, and showed him the leading marks, but it all fell on deaf ears. To all appearance, in that wind and sea, we were driving to destruction as the entrance to the river was masked, and nothing was to be seen ahead of us except a continuous line of breakers. This was the moment he chose to ask permission to go below and change as he wanted to come in 'respectable'. I told him to be quick about it and, as he was still below when I brought the marks on to clear the Mouthstone ledge, I shouted down the hatchway for him to come on deck at once. He replied, 'Coming, sir!' and then a figure appeared that resembled nothing so much as one of the ragged Guisers that street urchins hawk round on Guy Fawkes night. Standing up on the shock of red hair, at least two inches above the scalp, was a deerstalker cap, his body was encased in a very old-fashioned frock coat much the worse for dirt and wear, while the filthy tweed trousers were tucked into a pair of leather thigh sea-boots. His appearance gave me such a shock that for a moment of desperation I was inclined to cast *Dorothy* away on the bar rather than face the vessels in the anchorage. There was no time to do anything; we were already rounding Misery point, and it was essential that both of us should be on deck in order to pick a billet in the crowded river. Every eye was fastened on us as we swept past the shining yachts with their immaculate and grinning crews, and we had to run the gamut of the lot before we could find a billet below the hotel. No registration certificate, a disreputable looking ship, and a Guy Fawkes crew. My cup of humiliation was complete.

It may be thought that I have laid unnecessary stress on this question of appearance, and, in condonation, I should explain that I am a Victorian, and, as such, was brought up on the principle that no matter how empty your pocket it was necessary for the sake of one's proper pride to keep up appearances. What you did with improper pride, once you were satisfied you had acquired it, was not so specifically provided for. Also in those happy far-off days I belonged to a Service that, with a two-power standard of superiority, knew little about war and cared less. But it did know how a ship should be kept, and promotion to the higher ranks was the prerogative of those whose decks were the whitest, whose brass was the best polished, and whose perfectly enamelled paintwork showed a praiseworthy effort on the part of the commander and first-lieutenant to ensure that this result did not entail any addition to the naval estimates. A blister on the paint of a barbette was a much more serious blot on your scutcheon than a failure to hit a target at a thousand yards. I have known a commander look on an order to 'Out nets' as a sentence of professional death because the Admiral's inspection was due in a day or two, and it would be impossible to get the ship's side right again for at least a week. And many a first-lieutenant has carried a broken heart into the Coastguard because his pocket was not so deep as a paint-can. So it need not be wondered that I, too, was infected by this spit and polish bug, forgetting that the sea cares for none of these things, and that they are only bred in harbours which, in the words of the old salt, rot both ships and men.

Being yet under the bond of appearances the anchor was no sooner let go than I turned on Vincent and drove him below. There I called him every kind of ullage, and wound up by saying that he had made us the laughing-stock of the place. This really hurt him, but he had had no experience in yachts and made no reply. In some of the ships where he had served 'sauciness' would have been dealt with by a dose of 'belaying-pin soup'. But when I ordered him to take off the coat before I would allow him on deck again it was too much for his injured feelings. He told me that he had spent most of the money advanced to him in buying the outfit in order to come 'respectable', and he had taken as his pattern his last skipper, who had always gone ashore in a top hat and frock coat. By this time I was beginning to feel a bit ashamed of myself. A couple of hours before he had been in his own place at sea and worth more than a Jew's eye to me, and now, because he was ignorant of the niceties of yachting garb, I was behaving like an ungrateful cad. After he had removed the offending cap and coat we went on deck and stowed the canvas. When all was tidy he ran away the kedge, and I went below to change my rig.

I had no desire to appear on deck until the scandal of our arrival had died down, and I was glad to think that nobody I knew was likely to have seen us. But it is not easy to avoid recognition by someone if you have spent several years at a big public school and a university, and belong to the great sea service. Once when I thought I had reached the ends of the earth and that nobody was likely to know me, in Yokohama, I was astonished to get a note as soon as the ship was alongside the pier saying: 'Dear Muir, I have just heard by a side wind that you are on board the *Ancona*. Come and dine with me to-night at the Club on the Bund.' It was just the same in the Yealm. In a little while I heard a boat come alongside, but paid no attention as I thought it was the Coastguard, until there was a rapping on the deck and a voice shouted, 'Is Muir on board?' I put my head up and there was a lieutenant with whom I had been shipmates in a training brig. Common courtesy compelled me to ask him on board, and he sat on the settee opposite while I poured out the drinks. He eyed me over the top of his glass for a second, and then commenced the attack I was expecting.

'You've got a nice neck on you!'

I thought he was referring to the terrible exhibition coming in and was up in arms at once.

'What do you mean?'

'Aren't you glad you are alive coming in on a day like this? It's more than you deserve anyhow.'

'It was all right.'

'All right! Do you know that some people who were up on Battery Point thought you were bound to be wrecked, and the coastguards at Warren Point were getting the rocket apparatus out?'

'Rubbish!' I said. 'A lot of coddled old fools talking through the seat of their pants.'

'Well, if that's the way you look at it all I can say is that you must have a damned good ship, and that hand of yours must be a marvel to go to sea with you. There's hardly a ship here that does not want to go out, but the hands won't face it. I know of at least one owner who would be glad to swop with you.'

'Did you see the rig he was wearing?' I asked suspiciously. I thought he was pulling my leg.

'Yes. Poor devil! The last dry stitch he could muster, I suppose.'

'That was it,' was my mean answer, for which I could have kicked myself even as the words were leaving my mouth.

'He looked to me like a fellow who knew his job all right.' This is the highest praise that can fall from the lips of a naval officer.

Here was another vivid contrast with a vengeance. Instead of being the figures of fun I had imagined, we were the heroes of the anchorage. Later my friend left to return to the big yacht houseboat in which he was staying.

Not long after a dinghy came over from the houseboat with a note from the owner saying that, having heard from my visitor that everything on board my ship was soaking after our rough passage, he would be glad if I would come over and have supper with them, and the dinghy would wait for me. Whilst I was getting ready a seaman on my foredeck chatted with a seaman in the dinghy. I heard the end of the conversation as I came up. Vincent was remarking, much too casually, 'We could allus have got the jaws down on the boom you know,' and I guessed from his grin that he had been shamelessly exaggerating our prowess.

It was the local legend of this same prowess that was the cause of Vincent's first fall from grace. The next morning I rushed him up to Plymouth and, in a shop in the Barbican, he was rigged in a seaman's jersey and a pair of blue serge trousers. When a pair of white canvas shoes was added he became as vain and self-conscious as a girl of six in her first party frock. That same evening he asked whether he could have the dinghy for half an hour as his friend from the houseboat wanted to take him for a walk. Now, as everyone who visits the Yealm knows, there are a great many cosy wayside inns in the villages of Newton Ferrers and Noss Mayo about half a mile from the ferry landing place, and I think the nearest of these was the limit of the walk. At any rate the half-hour had more than quadrupled itself before I was roused from sleep by hearing Vincent hoisting the dinghy in the davits, and it could not be said that it was being done in a smart and seamanlike manner. However, I did not think it was worth while saying anything about it, as I am one of those people who are strongly of opinion that employers have no right to dictate to their employees how they are to amuse themselves as long as their amusement does not interfere with their efficiency. But the next night when the same performance was repeated, with the addition that he came in to the saloon where I was sleeping to tell me all about it, I thought it was time to call a halt, and I gave him a highly moral lecture on the evils of strong drink. This had little effect, for the following night his comatose form was tenderly deposited on the foredeck by kindly hands, and the dinghy tied up astern. They must have been very quiet about it as I heard nothing until he was violently sick in the early hours of the morning. I then read him a lecture on the evil communications that corrupt good manners, and took him to sea as the easiest way of reforming him.

In the meantime he had touched me for another week's advance and was now ten days in debt to the ship. Nor, as he informed me, had he a single penny left in his pocket, so we were bound for Salcombe where I felt sure I could keep him out of the way of temptation. On the way he addressed me as 'Guv'nor', and when I objected explained that he had heard the other yacht hands in the Yealm calling their owners by this term, and in his ignorance he thought it was the correct one and was rather proud of its acquisition. I told him that I knew it was the name given to their owners by some yacht hands, but that they only did so behind their backs, and never when addressing them.

This worried him a bit, and after long and frowning deliberation he asked how he should address me. I told him there was nothing the matter with the 'Sir' he had used up to the present, but I think he came to the conclusion that this rather abrupt terminology was hardly respectful enough in my position of employer and yacht owner, and thereafter I became 'Guv'nor—or as I should say—Sir'.

V

Salcombe

MANY YEARS AGO when I was a small boy at school I was prone to giving numberless reasons for my misdeeds, in the hope that one of them at any rate would be found sufficiently convincing to avert the expected and deserved punishment. Sometimes the hoped-for result took place, but I was singularly unsuccessful with the English master, who prided himself on his logical faculties, and I often worried over, and suffered for, my lack of power to carry conviction as far as he was concerned. One day after spinning him a yarn so plausible that I almost believed it myself, instead of letting me off with the caution I half hoped for, he just smiled and shook his head while he reached for the tawse. 'My boy! One good reason for anything you may do is sufficient for any just man. If you give two or more as is your usual habit they must have been invented. Hold out your hand.'

In spite of this sound advice I am bound to admit that there were two good reasons for my projected stay at Salcombe. For one thing it is a quiet place where I could get some painting and varnishing done before I subjected my ship to the scrutiny of the naval friends I was bound to meet in the Solent. The other reason was that Salcombe had recently become the home town of two elderly female relatives, who were anxious to renew the admiration they had professed to entertain for me on the occasion of our last meeting some twenty years before, when I had entranced them by the manner in which I had said 'goo', and by the ardour with which I had covered their maiden cheeks with sticky kisses. In recent letters to my people they had expressed their admiration for the brilliant career, they seemed to be in no doubt, I was carving out for myself, although it had never struck me that way. I was only grateful to the fortune that allowed me to knock about the world at somebody else's (in this case the unfortunate taxpayers') expense; a hobby I could never have indulged in if the cost had to be borne by my own pocket. It had been delicately hinted to me that they were both old with much worldly wealth to bequeath, and there were few with a claim on them except grasping hangers-on. So I had received strict injunctions to call at the first opportunity on my return from foreign service.

Lest any should think that this was a case of a dashingly handsome young rascal, for ulterior motives, worming his way into the affections of two innocent old ladies, I must relate an incident of my service career. I had just joined a ship on a foreign station, and after reporting myself to the commander sat down in the casemate smoking-room to await my interview with the captain. A particularly ill-favoured youth who got up on my arrival gave an exclamation of delight and shook me warmly by the hand. 'Thank God there's another beggar in the ship uglier than I am! Now these devils will leave me alone.' I found out later that his nickname on board was Sally, after a well-known chimpanzee in the Zoo. I have only to add that the hope he so fervently expressed was fulfilled.

We had been late in leaving the Yealm, and there was much swell and little wind so that it was nearly sundown before we anchored on the bank in Salcombe harbour just opposite the Salcombe hotel. I went ashore at once and found a note in reply to the wire I had sent off before leaving the Yealm saying that I was expected to lunch at one o'clock on the following day. That would suit me admirably as we could start rubbing down in the morning, and Vincent could slap on the first coat of paint while I was lunching ashore. Everything seemed to be fitting in nicely, and I went to sleep feeling that the world was not such a bad place after all.

Next morning was bright and sunny, and Salcombe was looking—well, like Salcombe on a sunny morning. I will not attempt to describe it. If I manage to convey even a feeble idea of its beauty you will not believe me unless you have been there, and if you have you will know that I am attempting the impossible. With many a glance at the scene around us the routine work of tidying the ship up was completed as quickly as possible, and at ten o'clock

I extracted a golden sovereign from my scanty store and handed it over to Vincent with instructions to go ashore in the dinghy to Dornom's and return, with all haste, after buying half a gallon each of paint and varnish and two brushes. I remained on board to finish off the saloon as this was my down below job.

I came on deck in about half an hour and, as my merchant had not returned, got out some scrapers and sandpaper and began work on the teak coaming of the cockpit. The work was interesting and time passed quickly. A glance at the saloon clock showed that it was now getting on for twelve, and that soon I would have to knock off and dress for the lunch and approval inspection that awaited me. There were still no signs of Vincent when I finally came on deck, dressed in the modest fashion which I imagined would be my best passport to the good graces of the old ladies. But I was fated to have no lunch that day. In growing wrath it was driven in on me that my red-headed hand had gone on the bust and forgotten all about me and my engagement. I did my best by shouting to call the attention of someone, and get a passage ashore, but my voice failed to carry as far as the beach, and the only acknowledgment I got of my hailing was from a fisherman in a distant boat who waved a cheery hand, evidently under the impression I was telling him what a lovely day it was. One o'clock passed and I thought of the pleasure it would give me to cut the villain's throat to slow music, or perhaps 'something lingering with boiling oil in it' would suit the offence better. But, fume and swear as I might, there was apparently to be no release for me until Vincent awoke from his gin-sodden sleep, or the golden sovereign ran out, whichever should happen first.

It was well after four when I sighted the dinghy coming down Batson Lake propelled by a Vincent who must be very drunk indeed to judge by the erratic course he was making. He continually pulled the dinghy right round until it was facing in the wrong direction, and then drove away from the ship for some time before he recognized his mistake. At last he ran ashore on the mud, stood up in the boat, and tried to push her off sideways with an oar, like a Bank Holiday tripper. Leaning heavily on the oar he managed to push the boat from under him so that he overbalanced and fell into about a foot of muddy water. I was so angry that I could not laugh, although the entertainment was heartily appreciated by a crowd of shore loafers who had suddenly sprung from nowhere, as Vincent floundered in the mud retrieving the dinghy and paddle. In course of time, and after further divagations, he arrived alongside, and sat in the dinghy presenting a cheerfully drunken grin to my scowling greeting. As he was quite unfit to climb the ship's side without assistance I hove him on deck with considerable violence and, when I let him go, he collapsed across the cabin top and assured me 'I've brought the paint'.

He had brought the paint but not a penny of the nine shillings change I demanded. All of it had gone in establishing his reputation as the most free-handed sailor who had ever shed the light of his generosity on the thirsty long-shore loafers of Salcombe. I was furious, and told him that he was as good as sacked, and that he would have to go as soon as he had worked off his debt to the ship. All the time we were arguing I was mad to get ashore, and explain to the poor old dears why I had been unable to keep my luncheon appointment. He seemed to have sobered up a bit and, just as he was, I made him row me down to the Watchhouse steps. On arrival I gave him strict orders to come in for me at six, and in the meantime he was to clean himself up and swab out the dinghy. I then fairly ran and, as anyone who knows the hills of Salcombe can guess, arrived at my destination, dishevelled and panting.

An unconscionably long time after my ring the door was opened by an elderly housemaid who must have been brought up on a diet of which vinegar had been the main constituent. I suppose my breathless condition roused her suspicions as to my sobriety, or my efforts at explanation were too disjointed for her comprehension, and it was only after some adjustment of her first impressions that I was able to convince her that I had any right to be at the front door at all. I thought at one moment she was going to send me round to the back—not an unheard-of experience in my case. When I managed to gulp out my name and ask whether Miss Lavinia could speak to me in the hall she stopped sniffing and invited me to wait in the drawing-room. But the points where I had been in contact with the muddy dinghy dare not settle on fresh cretonnes, and my shoes were still squelching from the bilge water. Vinegar seemed to think that my refusal indicated there might be some sense in me after all, and in a few minutes the dearest old lady that ever lived was doing her best to make head and tail out of my confused apologies. I am sure that until her dying day she had not the faintest idea what I was driving at, but it was at least clear to her that, for good and sufficient reasons, I had failed to keep my engagement and that I was genuinely distressed about it. So she did the best she could and asked me to come the following day at the same time. I accepted with gratitude, apologized for my dreadful appearance and left.

After doing the little shopping that was necessary I went back to the Watchhouse steps. There was no dinghy and no signs of Vincent. It was no use shouting, but I gave him half an hour's grace, and then hired a shore boat whose owner gave me a lurid description of my hand's spree with which the whole town was ringing. 'Taking the bread out of decent men's mouths I call it, employing a man like that.' 'You can have the job if you like,' I offered. He started as if I had hit him. 'Me! I've done a lot of funny things in my life but I've never come down to that.' 'Do you know of anybody suitable?' 'Well, if you want somebody to sell your paint and stores and loaf about all day I can find you plenty.' 'Is that what you think of yachtsmen? I've always found them very decent fellows.' 'I've no use for yachtsmen, always asking you for a shove off to their boats, and never a penny in their pockets to pay you with.' Evidently, like lots of other people in the world, his rôle in life was that of destructive criticism which doesn't help much.

While I was standing up in the boat alongside, fishing in my pocket for his fare, I was subconsciously aware of a rhythmical rumbling sound that seemed to pervade the whole hull of the yacht. Although in time it became tolerable, if I kept both doors between the fo'c'sle and saloon shut, this was the first time I had heard Vincent snoring, and the sound was daunting. Sure enough he was stretched out on a locker and sleeping the sleep of advanced intoxication. I roused him by knocking his head against a bulkhead until he was semi-conscious, and then reviled him for his latest dereliction of duty in neglecting to meet me ashore, and wound up by telling him to pack up and clear out at once. This last was too much for his sense of justice. He sat up and with owlish gravity let me know how it looked to him: 'I done wrong this morning. Nobody can say you fairer than that, but you, you ain't fair and I'm disappointed in ye. Ye knew quite well when ye gave me these orders I wasn't hardly sober, and no fair man would expect a drunk man to remember all you said to me.' Having relieved his feelings he gave a sigh, stretched himself out on the locker again and, in two twinks, was sound asleep. For a second I felt like murder, and then the humour of the situation was too much for me. I retreated to the saloon and rolled on a settee helpless with laughter. At nine, as usual, he brought in my supper and cleared it away and, after the usual 'Any orders, sir?', said good night and turned in. What a head!

During the night I did a lot of intensive thinking before I went to sleep. When it came to a job of work Vincent was as good a hand as I was likely to find anywhere, and he was entirely lacking in the sophistication that made many yacht hands an anxiety to their owners. There were plenty of first-class industrious honest men who were reliable servants, but the difficulty was to get hold of one who was willing to act as single-hand. Social conditions make life on board a small yacht a dreary business for the lone hand, and most men are unwilling to take the job on especially if there is the amount of day and night sailing I wanted to indulge in. I was prepared to keep my red-headed drunkard but it must be on my terms, and I was doubtful whether he would agree to these terms when he heard them. In spite of his misdeeds I had considerable qualms about putting him on the beach without a penny, and it would take at least a fortnight before he had worked off his debt to the ship and had a few shillings due to him. I had made up my mind that willy-nilly he would have to accept my terms for that period of his service, and he might be brought to see the advantage of continuing it.

After he had cleared up breakfast I called him into the saloon and explained the arrangement I intended to make. In future when he went ashore he would be given one shilling. I was sure he could not get very drunk on that small sum even in pre-war days. I would keep an account book showing the amount due to him on one page, and on the opposite page would be shown the amounts advanced to him for which he would sign when he drew the money. He made no objection at all, and I need not have been so surprised at his compliance if I had known that this was the way in which he was paid when serving in schooners, the final settlement being made when he was discharged at the end of a voyage. Long afterwards he confessed that in his own mind he had been rather astonished at the ease with which he had been able to get money, and had felt sure that this kind of luck was too good to last.

This being off my mind I was ready to go ashore for lunch at the proper time. The vinegar-faced one admitted me a trifle less acidly than on the previous evening; in fact, I think she nearly smiled as she showed me into a huge drawing-room. 'The ladies have just come in from the garden and will be down in a minute. Will you please sit down?' I was quite willing to sit down, and made my way to a big settee at either end of which were curled up two enormous Blue Persian cats whose appearance and demeanour indicated, probably quite correctly, that they were worth their weight in gold. I sat down between them and attempted to make friends, but their contemptuous disregard only too clearly showed that, in their opinion, I was not even up to copper standard. The ladies came in just as I was considering what the effect on their tempers would be if I pushed the haughty aristocrats on the floor and took the comfortable corner seat.

I renewed my acquaintance with Miss Lavinia and was presented to Miss Hetty, the younger of the two, who was all feminine, while the elder represented the masculine element in the household. She it was who controlled the outdoor staff, while the younger had charge of the indoor domestic affairs. After we had joked over this admirable arrangement I was introduced to the cats by name, Timmy and Jenny. These, I was told, were only their pet names, their stud book ones being too clumsy for ordinary use. Jenny felt my masculine allure and looked as if I might improve on further acquaintance, but Timmy yawned disgustedly in my face. A gong was heard and both cats jumped down from the settee and headed the procession into the dining-room. My attention was called in awestruck tones to the intelligence displayed by the pets in recognizing so quickly that a meal was in the offing.

Behold us then seated at table. At the head of the table, and on my left, is Miss Lavinia, but intervening between us is a luxuriously upholstered high chair on which is perched Sir Timmy, licking his chops; on my right is Miss Hetty, who has a similar seat on her right supporting Lady Jenny. I was not allowed the comforting illusion that I was the principal guest, as the cats were served with saucers of milk before we began with soup. The next course was fish, and I made my first blunder. Timmy eyed the morsel on my plate and came to the conclusion that I had meanly abstracted a tastier portion than that already doled out to him. He dropped his head on the side of my plate and was just about to seize it with his teeth, but I was quicker than he was and shifted my plate out of his reach. There was a shocked exclamation from Miss Lavinia: 'But Timmy likes that piece! Doesn't he, darling?' And I'll be hanged if that pampered brute did not give a plaintive mew in reply. It was evident that both ends of the table considered that I had displayed extreme selfishness, and when I tried to cover up my error by saying I only did it to tease they were sure I was an unfeeling wretch as well. My plate was handed over to the cat with sympathetic murmurings: 'Did the horrid man want to tease um poor darling?' and the beast mewed agreement every time. A fresh plate and more fish were brought and the meal proceeded to its close. But there was a little cloud.

After lunch we walked in the beautiful terraced garden down to the water's edge where a very nice-looking varnished rowing boat was lying at a frape*. Again I made a mistake when I offered to take them out for a row. They could not have looked more horrified if I had tried to push them into the sea. It was explained that the boat had been supplied so that the gardener could take the maids out for a row in the evening, and that the old ladies never ventured in it as boats always capsized if you changed seats, and all the occupants were invariably drowned. After hastily assuring them that I had had no intention of changing seats the painful subject was dropped by mutual consent. But there was little doubt in my own mind that the visit was not the success that had

---

*   Anchored a few yards out, with a line to the shore for recovering the boat. —Ed

been hoped for by all of us. It was chiefly my fault as I had failed to recognize the cramped life the old ladies had led, and did not foresee and make allowances for their natural prejudices. They were charming to me when the time came for me to leave, and asked me to call before I sailed, which I duly did. A few years later some of the charities that have the wisdom to suggest legacies rather than gifts were rewarded with very generous bequests.

On board, the painting and varnishing were finished, and we took our departure from Salcombe. There was a light easterly air that petered out completely when we were well into the middle of West Bay, and all that night we crept slowly to windward in a dense fog. As we were well out of the way of the main Channel traffic the fog did not worry us much, but on several occasions the creaking of blocks, the sound of voices and a splash as a hull rolled by, told us that we were not the only sailing ship about. At dawn a fresh easterly breeze came up which steadily gained in strength until we were pitching violently into a short head sea, which made things very uncomfortable. On account of the haze that always accompanies an easterly wind we could not be sure of our position, but it was estimated as five miles due west of the Bill, and the character of the sea suggested the close proximity of the Race. Neither of us had the least desire to be carried through the Race in the flood which was shortly due. After a brief discussion I decided to clear out of that unpleasant locality while the ebb would allow us to do so. Both Lyme Regis and Bridport are bad harbours to make for, and Exmouth was the nearest that offered reasonable shelter. We put up the helm and squared away for Straight Point, and in the strong breeze made short miles of it. The bar was sheltered by the point so that entrance was easy, and soon we were tied up to a buoy in that part of the River Exe known as the Bight.

This was not the first time I had funked Portland Race. Those who make the passage nowadays with the aid of an engine, so that they can guarantee their arrival at the most favourable moment for getting round the Bill, can have little idea of the respect with which the sailing man treated the Race, admittedly the most dangerous place in the English Channel for a small ship. From a safe position on the Bill I have seen a coasting ketch founder in the

Race with the loss of all hands although the weather was quite moderate. No attempt at rescue was possible. My feeling of tragic helplessness on that occasion has only been equalled by that previous experience when I saw a steamer with an enormous deck load of timber get broadside on to the wind and sea in a North Sea winter gale, when it was only by clearing out of that area at once that we saved our own ship from being sunk by the floating balks of timber.

VI

Exmouth

E XMOUTH IS NOT A SATISFACTORY HARBOUR from the yachtsman's point of view. Although the entrance is fairly easy in fine weather, and with a flood tide, it is dangerous if the wind is blowing strongly on shore, especially on the ebb which runs very hard. At night time and round about low water it is difficult to enter without good local knowledge and, once in, you must lie in an unpleasant dock or out in the anchorage called The Bight. The latter place is a long row from the landing place, and communication may be impossible if there is a strong wind or tide against you. Under favourable conditions the scenery can be very beautiful, but usually the view across the Warren sands or up the estuary is dull and depressing. My intention was to get away as soon as the wind shifted, but easterlies may last a long time, and I was beginning to be anxious to make to the eastward as I was a long way from Chatham. Vincent's remark when the work of clearing up was completed and he had a chance of looking round filled the bill: 'Well, I don't know but what we was just as well where we was to.'

I had noticed a nice-looking cutter at moorings higher up in the Bight, and towards evening an elderly man got into her dinghy and rowed round my yacht. After taking a good look at her, and, I suppose, sizing up the owner as well, he remarked, 'That's a nice-looking boat you have got there.' There is only one reply to make to such a verdict, and it was duly forthcoming: 'Glad you think so. Come on board and have a look at her.' He had evidently been waiting for such an invitation because he hopped on deck at once and introduced himself. I took him for a prosperous business man of some kind, and one who had got on in the world, as neither his ship nor his clothing agreed with his accent or his manner of address. During the short time he was on board I would have liked him much better if he had not been so anxious to let me know of the many ways in which his ship was superior to mine. One's taste in yachts is governed by one's pockets and not by one's ideals. He asked me to return his call after supper when he would have much pleasure in showing me over his ship.

The brass-bound skipper received me at the gangway, and showed me into the saloon where my acquaintance had been making preparations for my reception. The array of bottles and glasses on the table would have rejoiced the heart of Vincent. Their effect on me was to produce a hasty series of negatives to the consternation of my host. He was so dismayed at this extraordinary behaviour on the part of a yachtsman that he swept the lot on to a sideboard, confided that he couldn't stand the stuff himself, called to his steward to bring some coffee, and produced cigars wrapped in tinfoil. He had another shock, and I was compelled to smoke my own cigarettes. It was only my insistence that prevented him from sending the steward a three mile pull to buy some.

The yacht was such as, in view of recent happenings, I would never be able to afford, but I was quite sincere when I congratulated him on being the owner of a very beautiful vessel. After the inspection we sat down in the saloon and I began to talk yachting, than which there is no more interesting topic under the sun. But my host betrayed very little interest, and had no real knowledge of the subject. Again and again the conversation languished whilst I strove to find something we could talk about, but he knew nothing about books, travel, London, or people. At last driven to desperation I thought he must be a beginner at the game, and had taken it up late in life as so many men do, and remarked:

'I suppose you are very fond of sailing.'

'Me! I don't like sailing. Ain't got neither the head nor the stummick for it.'

'What in all the world do you mean by keeping a big expensive vessel like this if you don't like yachting?'

He picked me up at once.

'Yachting! Oh, I likes yachting.' And while I was turning over in mind this alleged difference between yachting and sailing he went on reflectively: 'Yes, I likes yachting. You see, you meets such a nice class of gent.'

As I have always considered that the yachtsman is the best of all sportsmen in the highest sense of the word I agreed with his estimate of their good qualities, and waited expecting a story and in due course he unburdened himself. It was a pathetic tale of loneliness, common enough I have no doubt. By his own efforts, and when he was already elderly, he had risen from the ranks of the labouring classes to a position of great wealth in a cathedral city. As his riches increased the friends of his youth fell away from him, and the only other society in the city would have none of him socially, although they never forgot him when a subscription list was opened. After the death of his wife he was unutterably miserable, and fast becoming melancholic, when a chance acquaintance suggested that if he bought a yacht his summer evenings at any rate need never be dull for want of companionship. All he had to do was to go alongside any yacht and get into conversation with the owner. Yachtsmen had no side and didn't care a button who or what you were as long as you served the sea. He had followed this advice and had never been so happy since he had earned his bread by the sweat of his brow. He showed me his visitor's book, and a perusal of the names in it would have made the tenants of the Close sit up and take notice. Later he told me some incredible stories of the slights he had suffered at the hands of the Church, usually the womenfolk, and recounted with glee that since buying the yacht he had not paid a single penny in subscriptions. He was an interesting man, a kindly man, and a desperately lonely one.

I was finding out that Vincent had one of the characteristics of the deep-sea sailor that I had forgotten. He could go into a port and, provided he had no money to spend, would sit down quite contentedly without the faintest wish to go ashore. Nor did he have the least wish to learn anything about the beach — the only use he had for it was to make purchases or to make friends in the easiest of all club houses, the taproom. I believe that his original estimate of himself was correct, and that he was not a drunkard. If he got into bad company and fell, it was from weakness not vice. He could get his shilling to go ashore any time he liked, but he rarely took advantage of it, chiefly because he was unable to stand treat all round, a method of spending his money which seemed to afford him a tremendous amount of gratification. He loyally stuck to his bargain, and never asked me to increase the amount doled out to him. I suppose he must have received a certain amount of satisfaction from the thought of the large sum piling up for his final paying-off day. Two years later when the time came for us to part, as I was going to sea and the yacht was sold, I found that Vincent had a credit balance of over forty pounds. I had managed to get him a berth as quartermaster in a tramp steamer trading from London to the East, and when I told him how much was due to him I saw a glint in his eye as he thought how great a power he would be in the Commercial Road, where it would all vanish during the week that was to elapse before sailing. So I told him that the money was being sent by me to the Bank which is run by the Board of Trade for the benefit of merchant seamen. This was a bit of a blow to him, only slightly modified by the five pounds I handed to him for current expenses.

I did not hear from him for nearly two years, when he wrote and told me he was rapidly becoming a man of wealth in spite of himself. It seemed that his captain, finding that Vincent had a large sum already in the bank, took it into his head that this was his usual method of saving his pay and had allotted the whole of it to the bank, only reserving enough for the barest necessities, and certainly not sufficient to finance a binge. With his usual docile acceptance of his officer's decisions Vincent had agreed to this disposal of his money, and, as he was much too shy to make any effort at withdrawal, he had been living in almost penury while his bank balance accumulated. At the time he wrote, the amount was far beyond his wildest dreams of wealth, and the responsibility of so much money was terrifying him. He had the common belief of many of his class that banks were likely to diddle him as soon as the amount became worth their while. Apparently I had converted a free-handed drunkard into a compulsory miser, with all the miser's terrors, and I am not prepared to swear that the change was all to the good.

However, I wrote and told him to confide his difficulties to the local chaplain to the Missions to Seamen and follow his advice. I never heard from him

again, and I have reason to believe that he died in the East not long afterwards — sober but rich.

One day during the war I went for a walk from Inverkeithing to Aberdour,
and was accompanied part of the way by a drunken Scots navvy. He was a
magnificent figure of a man, and when we parted I said what a pity it was that
so fine looking a workman should be in such a condition. He pulled himself
up with drunken gravity and waved his right hand in the air: 'Why should I be
sober when I can be a king for half a crown?' As I did not know the answer I
said nothing, but it flashed across my mind that he had betrayed the secret of
Vincent's outbursts. Poor Vincent! I hope he has forgiven me for the numberless times I have stood between him and kingship.

The east wind was succeeded by a light northerly, so one lovely summer
morning before dawn we caught the last of the ebb and stole out into West
Bay in another effort at rounding the Bill. Progress was slow but the sea was
smooth and the air was warm, and Vincent found time hanging heavily on his
hands. He prepared the breakfast and cleared it away, washed the ship down
fore and aft, polished the brasswork, and then came and sat in the well beside
me where I was sitting idly smoking and pretending to steer. He offered to relieve me, but I preferred to carry on so that I might have the better excuse for a
sleep in the afternoon. For a time we yarned about nothing in particular until
he woke me up effectively by asking:

'Have you ever been on the boards, sir?'

As my only appearance in that capacity had begun with an alleged recita-
tion and had ended with a howl when I was about ten I was able to say, truth-
fully enough, that I had never attempted to emulate Henry Irving. He seemed
disappointed and waited a little before he went on: 'Funny things actors and
actresses.'

Thinking to pull his leg I said: 'Have you ever been on the boards, Vincent?'

He took my chaff quite seriously. 'Oh yes, I have been on the boards all
right.'

This was quite amusing. 'Where was that, Vincent?'

'I was on the boards at Drury Lane.'

For a moment I was taken all aback. Anything less like a Drury Lane actor than my redheaded hand could not be imagined.

'What in all the world were you doing there?'

If his complexion had been less gingery I would have imagined that he was blushing, and when he answered it was almost coyly: 'I was the monkey in the Christmas pantomime.'

I am glad to recollect that Vincent took my unrestrained laughter as a tribute to his former greatness. But the more I thought about it the more I was convinced that the man who had chosen him for that particular part was a genius. He had a very powerful long body and very short legs, while his gait had struck me on several occasions as being peculiarly simian. He explained that he had an uncle and aunt who were much in demand as animal performers at the pantomimes, and who were always sure of an engagement at Drury Lane. During one of his spells on shore his uncle had recognized his dormant talent and insisted on including him in the troupe. He had given it up because he could not stand the smell of himself in the monkey's costume. At least so he said, but I am sure the real reason was that the sea had suddenly demanded his allegiance again. He had never gone back, but no prima donna recalled with more delight the applause of her sophisticated audience than Vincent remembered the hysterical cheering of the children when he bounded on the stage. He insisted on showing me how he did it, and I thanked my stars that we were alone on the broad ocean or there might have been complications and misunderstandings.

Away on the horizon the wedge of Portland was beginning to take definite shape.

VII

The Race

I HAVE ALREADY SAID SOMETHING about Portland Race and the anxiety felt
by the small ship sailor when it is necessary to round Portland Bill in the
course of a voyage. The Race, which can be, and very often is, the most wildly
tempestuous area in British waters, extends for two miles to the south of the
Bill, and in moderate weather it is highly dangerous for a small vessel to pass
through it, while in a gale it has been known to sink ocean-going steamers. Between the Race and the Bill there is usually an eddy of comparatively smooth
water, and for three hours out of the twelve a small ship can dodge the Race by
rounding the Bill close inshore. During these three hours going east the tide
runs down the west side of Portland, round the pitch of the Bill and up the
east side of Portland, and will carry you into the safety of Portland harbour
and Weymouth bay. Part of the stream on the west side will carry you right
into the Race, and approaching the Bill from the west, you must cross this
part of the stream well to the north of the Bill where it has little strength.
Nearing the Bill it rapidly increases in speed until, close to the Race, the rate
of six or seven knots is so powerful that, once in its grip, no small sailing craft
can hope to escape.

I hope this explanation is clear enough to allow the reader to understand
the difficulties. Speed in a sailing ship is dependent on the wind, which is notoriously fickle in direction and irregular in strength. One hour the ship may
be doing five knots and the next three or even less, while, if the wind dies
away, she is completely at the mercy of the tide. The passage to the Bill from
any of our western ports is a long one, and all sorts of things may happen to
prevent arrival at the desired spot, a couple of miles to the northwest of the
Bill, so as to take advantage of the three hours during which the inside pas-

sage through the eddy is reasonably safe. To add to the anxieties it is well known that as a ship approaches Portland sudden shifts of wind and flat calms are frequent, and, should the latter take place before crossing the tide at the right spot, there is no hope of passing through into the eddy or attempting the alternative of standing out to sea for several miles and avoiding the Race altogether. The ship will, for a certainty, be carried through the Race, but during neap tides and in calm weather that will be done with but little risk. At spring tides or in blowing weather the danger is very great.

As we sailed along on that glorious summer day I explained to Vincent just what the risks were but found that, as always when navigation or pilotage were touched upon, he had not the faintest interest in the subject, and was prepared to believe that I knew all about it. He was going to leave that kind of thing to me while he got on with the duties that pertained to his own department. He knew nothing about the Race except wild tales of its violence in bad weather, as all the ships he had sailed in gave it a wide berth in their voyages up and down the Channel. I tried to explain the tides, to be met with the reply: 'I don't hold with tides. Give me a fair wind and the tides won't matter.' The answer was easy enough: 'Let's hope we shall have a fair wind, then.'

Although I had allowed over twelve hours to do the passage of thirty-three miles from Straight Point to the Bill, the tide had turned to the east and was running hard as we closed with Portland, and we had missed the best time of all for rounding, i.e., slack water. This did not worry me much, as the breeze was still strong enough to force me across the south-going tide and into the section of the current I wanted to carry me round the Bill. Where we were sailing the water was perfectly smooth, but I had forgotten that this was due to the fact that we were under the lee of the land, and I did not know there was still a fairly big popple off the Bill as the result of the recent easterly breezes. Therefore, it did not cause me any anxiety when I found that I could no longer keep the pitch of the Bill well open of my lee bow, and knew for a certainty we were bound to go through the Race. In spite of it being Springs I was of opinion that it merely meant a bit of a struggle before I could get free of the tide and work my way into Portland whither I was bound. I did rather wonder what the Race would be like at Springs in a flat calm, as the sailing directions were, as usual, gloomy about one's prospects if one were caught in my present position.

The wind died away completely and, in the distance, I could see a line of broken water which seemed to be racing towards us with appalling speed. One glance at it was enough for Vincent, and he began with all haste to get the cover on the fo'c'sle hatch, stow the foresail, and let fly the jibsheets. I closed the saloon hatch and hardened in the main and mizen sheets to prevent the booms crashing about. The sails, of course, were useless. My biggest anxiety was the cockpit, which could hold over a ton of water. Although the floor was watertight it opened directly into the accommodation below by means of folding doors, and there were entrances to the lockers under the side decks. Two small scuppers drained into the sea from the aft corners of the floor, but they acted very slowly, and would be almost useless to get rid of the water if the cockpit filled.

As I watched the rapidly approaching crest it collided with another running at right angles to it, causing a wave about ten feet high to shoot into the air and fall back into the sea again with a resounding smack—a grim enough warning of what was going to happen if we collided with it ourselves. I knew it would not take much pounding like that to smash our thin decks in, and the next wave would finish us. I had no time to dwell on this interesting subject as we suddenly slipped sideways down a smooth incline of water similar to those you can see in any river when the stream glides quickly over a submerged stone. At the bottom of such an incline you will find a curling edge of spray on the top of a perpendicular wave. This was the crest we had seen in the distance, and in a second we were swept into it and collided with a whack which I thought must have broken half the ship's frames. I suppose some water had got into the cockpit because Vincent, after vainly attempting to get me to hear something, dived for the pump spear which was kept in a side locker.

The noise of the Race, its most distressing feature, was so great that it was impossible to understand one another's shouts, and we had to converse by signs. I was holding the tiller rather loosely in my right hand, as I feared if

I held it rigidly the impact of the waves on the blade might smash the rudder. We had buzzed completely round by this time and were heading for Exmouth again, when a sneaking beggar of a wave caught the rudder and drove the tiller into my ribs with such force that I knew exactly where it had hit me for a month afterwards. Water was coming in over both sides and ends at the same time; alternately we were thrown up on a pinnacle of sea so that we could see the Race spread out beneath us; then we would fall with a crash into frothy water whose buoyancy was so feeble that we sank in it until our decks were below the level of the sea. An extended hand from Vincent made me look astern just in time to see the dinghy turn a somersault and then float bottom up. Every few seconds the yacht dived head foremost into a breaker, burying herself up to the mast, and then threw the bowsprit, twanging and vibrating like a harp string, high in the air.

The most serious blow of all came when we were about half-way through the Race. A pyramid of water was playing on our beam, at one moment approaching and the next running parallel with our course, almost as if it were playing cat and mouse with us and enjoying the rôle of cat. For a little I thought we might escape, and the same idea seemed to occur to it as well for, suddenly, it reared higher and then made straight for our beam with added speed and fury. It caught us just abaft the channels. The lower part of the wave was stopped by a sickening blow on the hull, but the momentum of the upper part carried it clean across the ship and into the luff of the mainsail half-way up the mast. The force of the impact heeled us over to an angle of forty-five degrees and I expected that the vessel would capsize or that the mast would go. But all that happened was that as soon as the plane of the sail was at a suitable inclination the wave rushed up the sail, over the gaff, and into the sea again.

That was the end of our troubles, or perhaps what followed suffered by comparison with that appalling blow. After another short period of buffetings and drenchings we were through the Race and floating in smooth water again. Floating? Yes, but a bit deep. So deep that I tore open the cabin slide to see what the state of affairs was down below. Sure enough the swish-swash showed that the water was well above the cabin floor, and half the contents of the lockers seemed to be swilling about in it. Vincent said nothing, but in less than no time the pump was going, and it looked sinister to me that, for the first time, it drew without priming. As the bottom of the yacht was cemented well up it did not take an awful lot of water to show above the cabin floor, but until we had pumped her dry it was doubtful whether she was leaking badly or whether the water had arrived by a legitimate route. Ten minutes' hard work at the pump calmed our fears, and as the last drop of water went over the side as clean as when it came in I said: 'You must have made a good job of cleaning these bilges in Salcombe, Vincent.' He looked up with a grin, panting from his exertions at the pump: 'If I'd known we was coming here I'd have saved my trouble.'

Although, once clear of the Race, there was quite a nice breeze, we were well past the Shambles lightship before I was able to get out of the strength of the tide and work into Weymouth bay. Then we took stock of the damage after righting and emptying the dinghy. A torn mizen and a drenched saloon were the worst items. It was midnight before we had worked into Portland harbour and anchored close to Castletown pier. After a hasty stow we got to bed, and all night long I was chased by pinnacle waves.

Early next morning a pilot on his way to his ship stopped for a yarn. 'It must have been you that some of our people saw in the Race last evening.' 'I expect it was. We came through the Race.' I thought he might want to tell us what fine seamen we were and what a good ship we must have, but the only bouquet he threw was: 'You may thank your lucky stars you came through when the Race was quiet. You'd never have lived else.'

Vincent waited until he had gone. 'Quiet, was it? Why, I couldn't hear my-self speak. He don't know what he's talking about.'

'That is just the point,' I said. 'He does know and he's quite right. The Race was quiet.'

'Well, keep me away from it. I don't want another hour like that for a long while.'

'Hour!' I said. 'The Race isn't more than a mile wide this weather and the tide runs at least six knots. We weren't in the Race for more than ten or twelve minutes.'

But this was too much for Vincent's credulity, and the longer we sailed together the longer became the alleged time we spent in the Race until it had gained fantastic proportions in his mind. But for over twenty years I took his advice and kept away from it, and it was not until I owned a yacht with a reliable auxiliary motor that I failed to give the Race a berth of five miles on my passages up and down Channel. The Service allows you to make one mistake, but a repetition of the same mistake argues that you are a fool. I have always held that drowning is as good a death as any other, but I should hate to think as the water closed over my head for the last time that I was getting the death I deserved because I was a fool.

VIII

A Good Run

WE SPENT A DAY OR TWO in Portland, and then made a passage to Cowes which took exactly thirty-six hours for the forty-four miles as there was hardly a breath of wind the whole way. In the Solent we did all the usual things: ran ashore on the Shrape mud going into Cowes because my draught was only five feet, and I thought I could play hanky-panky with the deep channel; anchored in Portsmouth harbour in a forbidden area, and were chased out of it by the King's Harbourmaster (as an old shipmate he need not have been so infernally jubilant about catching me out); ran ashore in the Beaulieu River, and introduced Vincent to some of the joys of kedging off unsuccessfully on a falling tide; in spite of our efforts to avoid it, got in the way of some racing craft and learned, to my disappointment, that there was some vituperation I did not know, but could readily remember for use on a future occasion; cleared out of Stokes Bay in the middle of the night for a southerly gale, and learned to my surprise that there is not a single good safe harbour for small craft in the Solent that can be entered in the dark; and finally anchored off Stevens' yard, just above the Royal pier at Southampton, with five days of my leave still to go and two hundred odd miles from my destination. In accordance with a private arrangement made before starting on my expedition, I went ashore to the post office and sent a reply paid telegram submitting that forty-eight hours extension of leave might be granted to me. A few hours later the answer arrived and was handed to me. 'Extension of leave not approved.' That was a blow as I had been confident of getting the extra leave when I sent off the telegram. Something must have gone wrong, and there was nothing to do except obey my orders. 'Growl you may but go you must.' With luck I might be able to take the ship back with me, so we got busy although there was a lot to be done before we could make a dash for it.

I went ashore to buy provisions while Vincent filled up with water. We had made up our minds that we would remain at sea if the weather were light until we arrived at Chatham; if we made good progress we might call at Dover. Vincent's solution of the problem of making passages in the shortest possible time was to keep going, and I quite agreed with him. We turned in late but all ready to get under way at seven the next morning as this time would give us the most favourable tide.

We were wakened at dawn by the motion of the ship and the noise of the wind, both sufficiently assertive to assure us that we were not fated to suffer the annoyance of a flat calm at any rate. A glance outside showed the wind was fair and that there was plenty of it. We discussed whether it was wise to start, and decided that it was worth while having a look at it. The first twenty miles would be in sheltered water, and we could come back if the wind were too strong for us. After that—well, there was Dover, a hundred miles away. Newhaven as a port of refuge was not considered such by us.

What with the breakfast, weighing the kedge, hauling down a reef in the main and staysails, securing everything for sea, getting the canvas up and the anchor weighed and secured, it was nearly nine before we got away and tore down Southampton Water, the shores of which were invisible in the heavy rain squalls. It soon became evident that we would have to pull down the second reef and shift the second jib for the spitfire. We nursed her into the shelter of Osborne Bay and shoved her up in the wind. After stripping off our oilies and sea-boots we effected the desired reduction of canvas, had a further bout of securing, put her in front of it and let her go. About that period there was a saying, 'Klondyke or bust'. For us it was a case of 'Dover or bust'.

I had intended to take the Looe channel, and with that idea had read up the sailing directions in the most depressing volume the Admiralty have ever issued from the Hydrographic department. As we swept past Ryde Pier I recalled with gloom that 'The Looe channel, lying as it does within the whole line of dangers, barred at its narrow western entrance by heavy overfalls, is

only adapted for those possessing local knowledge except under very favourable circumstances.' I had pretty good local knowledge and I knew that, in this
weather, these overfalls would make Portland Race, as we had experienced
it, look like a millpond in comparison. The only alternative was to go round
the Owers, and Vincent was able to cheer me up by telling me of some of his
exploits in that unpleasant locality. On top of that we were going to add ten
miles to what was threatening to be a poisonous passage.

There was nothing for it but to shape a course for the Nab lightship from
the Warner. As we passed close to her she sent up a string of flags which I was
too frightened to read so I ignored them. One thing I do know. It was not the
signal T C Z or, in other words, 'I wish you a pleasant voyage'. They did not
seem to be having any too good a time themselves and, 'Nasty job they have in
these 'ere lightships,' remarked Vincent, 'I wouldn't take one of them on, no
not for nothing I wouldn't.' The Owers lightship when we passed her, plunging and straining at her anchors, and shipping it green over her bows, also
sent up a string of signals to us. In fact, as Vincent commented: 'Quite chatty,
them fellows. I suppose it's a bit dull for them out here.' I did not say anything
as I had a shrewd idea they were telling me things I'd rather not know, so
the code book was left in its locker. Soon they were lost to sight in the murk
astern.

By this time we had lost the shelter of the Island. The wind did not seem
quite so strong, and since we had dropped the Owers the sea had become more
regular, and the ship easier to hold. She was running without the wild gyra-
tions from side to side that had made a spinning top of the compass, and making it necessary to steer by sight and guess. If we were to make a decent course
to Beachy Head, thirty-six miles away, and not pile up on the Seven Sisters
or the Varne shoal, it was essential that the compass should have a sense of
duty and responsibility. With the easier steering and the steadier compass all
our difficulties seemed to vanish, and there was a feeling of intense exhilara-
tion in the way the ship rose and fell to the huge combers coming up astern. I
only looked aft once, and then I recognized the wisdom of the old sailing-ship
skippers who boxed their helmsman in so that they could only see ahead. The

sight was terrifying and yet somehow queerly exciting and satisfying. Vincent grinned his monkey's grin when I hastily turned my head round and glued my eyes on the compass.

We were eating up the miles, and so far everything was all right, but as soon as the tide turned against us the sea would rapidly get much worse and the real trial would begin. I told my doubts to my companion, but he just laughed and refused to meet trouble half way. 'Never mind the tides. Gimme a fair wind.' 'You've got it, you ronyon*'. He grinned more cheerfully than ever.

As evening came on the wind blew harder than ever, the tide began to ebb and the sea lost its regular character. Where it had sprayed it now soused us. The main boom was tripping in the water on the lee side, which added greatly to the difficulty of steering and kept me on tenterhooks in case of a jibe. The ship was becoming hard pressed, and it was time to give her some relief. I was nervous about rounding her up in the wind, so we did what we could to ease her by tricing up the tack of the mainsail and stowing the reefed staysail, but these measures were of only temporary benefit. We would have to get her round somehow, and at last, with my heart in my mouth or my boots, I really don't know which, I watched for a smooth and put the helm down while Vincent rounded in on the main-sheet. She came up all right, but at the end of the manoeuvre hit the sea a biff that sent a cloud of spray over us and effectually completed our soaking. Vincent shook his fist at it, and then we stripped the oilies and got on with the work. It was very heavy labour with the canvas like pasteboard and the reef points like wood. In the meantime we were astonished at the quietness with which she lay. With the spitfire jib aback and the helm a little down she gently bowed the sea and was perfectly dry and comfortable. So when Vincent suggested that we should get her going again I refused to listen. 'Not before we have had something to eat and a shift into dry clothes.'

In the gathering darkness we dived below to such comparative comfort as I am rarely likely to experience again. We had had nothing to eat since break-

---

*   Mangy or scabby creature (archaic).—Ed

fast, and had been soaked to the skin for hours, and we fairly gloated over the snug dryness of the saloon. Vincent sat on the floor with the Primus between his knees and boiled the water, while I pulled off my wet clothing and chucked it in a heap into the fo'c'sle. Then I dressed and luxuriated in the warm dry clothing than which nothing is more acceptable when you are wet and chilled. Vincent changed while I took his place on the floor and finished the boiling. We drank pints of scalding hot tea, ate our fill, and then insisted on a smoke before we faced the beastly night outside again. But we dare not stay too long in that blissful comfort because we knew we should drop off to sleep if we did. As it was it took a violent effort to drag ourselves away. Vincent's 'We mustn't waste a fair wind' took us on deck in a hurry.

Off once more, with Beachy showing a little on our lee bow, just where we had wanted to see it, and soon we were galloping past the Royal Sovereign, held by the tide broadside on to the sea and rolling damnably. The wind had taken off a bit but the sea was vicious and the compass useless. With the loom of the coast towns to guide us, Wee Willie Winkie on the point of Dungeness hove in sight long before his more august brother, and all was well as far as our course was concerned. Just as dawn was breaking, and a horrid high dawn it was, we rounded the Ness, and out from behind it came the big Dutch pilot schooners that had been sheltering under its lee for the night. Still the strong wind drove us on, but to the east of Dungeness the sea rapidly subsided and all was peace and comfort. The harbour at Dover was not completed but we passed in through the western entrance, had a look at Dover Wick and saw little chance of getting a billet in that crowded anchorage, carried on and dropped our anchor a little to the east of an old promenade pier which used to stand in the bay in front of the town. We had taken exactly twenty hours from Southampton, one hundred and twenty miles away.

Where we lay we rolled and rolled, but no roll on the sea could have disturbed the sleep Vincent and I lay down to when we had finished, and cleared up, breakfast. We were still rolling when we woke about two p.m., and soon the ceaseless motion became maddening. It was useless to think of leaving before dawn the following morning as I had no wish to attempt the navigation of the Thames in the dark. At last we got desperate and decided to spend an hour or two ashore. We dressed, the ladder was put over the side, and Vincent held the boat to the ship's side to let me get in. I had got into the boat but was still holding on to the gangway stanchion when the yacht lurched heavily towards me, and the gunwale of the dinghy got under the ladder and was forced under the water. Here was a mess up. I was standing in the submerged dinghy holding on to it with my toes and still having a grip of the stanchion. Vincent had been thrown into the water and, as he could not swim, was running considerable risk of drowning. My difficulty was to clear up the mess without losing Vincent, the dinghy, or the ship. Somehow with my right hand I managed to grab Vincent and haul him towards the channels, and I do not think that even in his stage days he ever made a quicker come back than when he clambered on board. The rest was easy, but the job of getting the water out of the dinghy was a teaser on account of the heavy rolling. After we had changed we got ashore, but not in the same condition to delight the eye as when we started.

IX

Back Again

IF WE WANTED TO GET TO CHATHAM within the forty-eight hours that remained of my six weeks' leave it was necessary to take the ebb tide from
Dover up to the North Foreland, and there catch the first of the flood up the
Thames. I calculated that I must allow four hours for the passage to the Foreland, and that meant leaving at 3 a.m. In the lovely summer morning that succeeded the gale it was sheer delight to get away from the miserable rolling in
Dover's so-called harbour. There was a light north-west wind, a slight haze,
and a golden halo to the eastward that made the sunrise lighting up St. Mar-
garet's Bay one of the most beautiful I have ever witnessed. Once round the
South Foreland the sea was perfectly smooth as we passed Deal and headed
for the Gull lightship, barely visible in the morning mist.

The mysterious vague yearnings aroused in the soul of every man by scenes
of great natural beauty were interpreted by Vincent in a strictly literal sense,
and he disappeared into the fo'c'sle and soon gave evidence of the depth to
which his feelings had been stirred by the aroma of coffee and bacon wafted
aft from the open hatch. By and by he pushed up his head and surveyed the
scene, prospective and actual, with undisguised satisfaction. 'Breakfast will
be ready in ten minutes,' he said. 'Wish there was a little more wind. We're
going to miss that tide at the North Foreland you're so keen about.' He came
on deck to alter the trim of the jib sheet, and when he had got it to his liking
stood gazing at something that had caught his eye right ahead of us.

'What's caught your vagrant fancy now, Vincent?' I asked lazily.

'Can't make it out properly from here, sir. Looks to me like a rowing boat
with folks in it that doesn't know how to row.'

'Have a look at them through the glasses.'

He took a long look and then exclaimed: 'It's a crowd of little girls in a shore boat.'

'What in all the world are they doing out here at six in the morning?'

'I don't know, but if they are not in trouble they very soon will be by the way they're rowing. They don't know nothing about it. Better keep away a bit, sir, and we'll pass close to them.'

I did as directed and in a short time saw the object of his anxiety. In a big heavy rowing boat were half a dozen girls of fourteen to sixteen, and it was obvious that they were ignorant of the faintest rudiments of oarsmanship. The only result of their efforts was to make the boat turn round in circles, and before we got up to them I thought they were going to capsize the boat in an attempt at recovering a lost oar. Except for the two who were rowing, who were very hot and bothered, they were all very cheery, shouting morning greetings and waving their hands to us.

I looked around, but there was nothing else in sight but a distant cargo steamer. What was this crowd of incompetents doing over a mile off shore at this time in the morning in a boat they were quite incapable of handling? The tide was running strongly to the northward, and they could never get that great lumbering boat anywhere near the shore again. If the breeze freshened as we hoped it would they would be carried on to the Goodwins for a certainty. It didn't take me more than a minute to make my decision and I called to Vincent: 'I'll run alongside them and you stand by to get hold of their painter.' I altered course and bore straight down on them. Some of the girls shrieked as if they thought we were going to run them down, but Vincent cleverly fended the boat off, grabbed hold of the painter, and made the boat fast alongside.

The younger girls looked on this as an added amusement to their morning outing, but the eldest girl was furious and demanded to know what we meant by interfering with them, with a threat of reprisals at the first opportunity. I paid no attention to her but asked one of the others where they had come from. She said Deal. The first girl was still volubly regretting that no gentleman was present to teach me my place, and it was time to take her in hand.

'Have you enough sense to understand that there is no chance of your getting this boat back to Deal while the tide is running against you, and that if the wind gets up you all stand a risk of being drowned.' She blenched a bit at that, and one of the children began to cry. I went on. 'Of course I can't compel you to take help if you refuse it, but if I leave you you will be in considerable danger. Take my advice and come off your high horse and be thankful there is someone to pick you up.' At the end of my speech there were more howls and the others reproached the older girl for having tempted them to this early morning adventure. It seemed that they had all come down from town the night before for the week-end, that none of them had ever been in a boat in their lives except the wrathful one, and her only experience had been trailing round the Serpentine. They had been so excited over their arrival at the sea-side that they could not sleep and had come down to the beach at dawn. They had found the boat which the united strength of the lot of them had just been able to push into the water. The tide and their rowing had done the rest. I think it must have been the smell of my coffee that did the trick, but suddenly my enemy disappeared behind a languishing smile.

'Oh! I am so hungry,' she said.

There was only one thing to be said. 'So am I. Come on board and have some breakfast.'

Vincent dived below to do more cooking than he ever did again while he was in my service. While that crowd of kids investigated every nook and cranny of the ship and were generally having the time of their young lives, I was wondering what was the best thing to do with them. Finally, I decided to work across the southern edge of the Brake sand into the Ramsgate channel, and then heave-to in the Old Cudd and send Vincent ashore with them at Ramsgate. From there they would have to find their own way back. As it was, the delay was going to make me miss the tide up the Thames even if I managed to struggle round the North Foreland. The wind was still fitful and dying away, while the girls stuffed themselves in the saloon and Vincent waited on them. Shortly after I had finished the meal which had been brought to me in the cockpit during one of Vincent's respites from more urgent appetites, I was joined by the haughty Miss Geraldine, who had evidently been doing something to her hair. I hoped she had not been using my brushes.

'I must apologize if you thought I was rude when you first spoke to us. You see, I did not know that you were a gentleman and that this was a yacht. I thought you were just common sailors.' Her best society manner was amusing and not very convincing, while her expressive glance at my sea-soiled suit showed that in her eyes it had no claims to a Bond Street origin.

'But there is no such thing as a common sailor.'

'Well, that man you call Vincent, he's just a common sailor, isn't he?'

I grinned as I remembered the vision of Vincent entering the Yealm.

'No, I should hardly call Vincent a common sailor.'

'Well, he calls you "sir", and he told me you were a naval officer.' Coyly, 'You know, I have never met a naval officer before.' She sighed as she looked back on a vista of weary years during which this boon had been denied her. Then, eagerly: 'Will you send me your photograph in uniform?'

I explained that for obvious reasons I rarely had my photograph taken. The reply was scarcely flattering.

'The uniform would be all right and I could show it to my friends.' Another scalp, I supposed. She might be only the sixteen she looked, but she had considerably more sophistication than any of the others who joined us in the well at that moment and compelled a change in the conversation. They were just like a crowd of young puppies, and were chaffing Vincent unmercifully about his top-knot, much to his sheepish delight.

I made Miss Geraldine promise to telegraph her people as soon as she got ashore, as the loss of the boat must have been discovered by this time, and they would be wild with anxiety. She said she would do so, with more than a hint that my wishes were her laws. When I suggested that they might not have enough money for the journey back to Deal she loftily assured me that her parents always kept her well provided with spare cash and she had plenty. As we drew near to Ramsgate harbour I saw a small fishing boat going in, hailed them and gave them a short account of what had happened. In return for a modicum of filthy lucre they promised to put the girls ashore, who were bundled into the boat by Vincent before they fully recognized what was happening. My last impression was of Miss Geraldine standing up in the stern of the retreating boat and shouting out: 'You've forgotten to give me your name and address.' I hope she was able to hear my answer: 'And you have forgotten to give me yours.' 'Whew!' said Vincent as they disappeared behind the piers. 'That was a crowd and a half. There ain't more bacon left than for just one more breakfast.' He had rather a hectic time with some of the young monkeys when they were washing up in the fo'c'sle, as they insisted on having a lock of his hair as a memento. They had never seen such a lovely colour in all their lives.

As I expected, this diversion had taken so much time that we missed our tide round the Foreland, and it was only after a deuce of a struggle that we managed to enter the Thames. Then began a wearisome beat with a failing wind through the Horse and Gore and into the Overland channel. The turn of the tide found us off Herne Bay, and at sunset we anchored close to the Columbine buoy as the wind had gone and the weather was hazy. Night fell and we slept peacefully. There was no need to get up early as the tide did not serve until ten. With it under us, and a nice little west wind, I picked up my moorings at Chatham with eighteen hours of my leave still to go.

X

Holland

I WANTED TO CRUISE IN HOLLAND; in fact, one of my reasons for buying *Dorothy* was that she was suitable for the job. When I asked Vincent what he thought about it, he could only give me the undesired and irrelevant information that both baccy and beer were cheaper in that enlightened country, and that therefore it more nearly approached his idea of Paradise than this tax-ridden Empire was ever likely to attain. The shilling arrangement I have previously mentioned had worked all right, but the greater purchasing power of that small coin in Holland may have had something to do with his enthusiasm for the projected destination. He wound up his arguments in favour of going by the statement, entirely unsupported by any trustworthy evidence, that it was a little bit of all right. My own inclinations were due to the enthusiasm of a book called Thorpe's *Guide to the Dutch Waterways*, which had been my favourite mental pabulum during several winters. The book had advised the avoidance of difficulties by the ownership of a yacht having a draught of not more than four feet, and power of some kind. The draught of my ship was five feet, and I had no auxiliary power. Still, I thought we might manage. This was before the days in which to have no engine was to label yourself either as a crank or a back number. Between ourselves, I strongly suspected I was both.

There was very little to do in order to get ready. The ship was lying at her moorings fitted out, so there were only provisions to be got on board and Admiralty permission obtained to cruise in foreign waters. Both were easy, and one Saturday we left Chatham late on the ebb and anchored in Queenborough after dark, having had all the wind we wanted on the way down. That night it blew a gale, and we spent most of the dark hours trying to keep our sheering vessel from violent contact with the barges which were running in for shelter. By Monday the gale had blown itself out and, on top of the flood, we began to beat down the Swale against a light northwest wind. When we were almost clear, and in another five minutes would have had the whole width of the Medway for our manoeuvres, the Flushing steamer came up the narrow channel. It was necessary to give her all the room possible, and I gave her a bit more than that and went aground on the mud. Like most sailing men I rarely run ashore except in my home port. We did all the usual things to get the ship off, but the ebb had started and there we remained until the next high water, so we came back to Queenborough for the night. By this time the search for Holland and the Golden Fleece seemed much on a par in my mind, and when it blew another gale that night, instead of thanking my stars that I was not hove-to off the West Hinder, I was moaning like a fractious seagull.

However, we got away next morning, and in light airs managed to make Ramsgate and tie up in the west gully just before dark. That would have been all right if it had not been for a lunatic on board the yacht lying between us and the quay. He had us up three times because he thought our cross-trees were fouling his. They weren't, but he had a wife on board who was nervous. As all yachtsmen know, the dues at Ramsgate are not cheap, but when he rapped us up for the last time at dawn we felt, for the first time in yachting history, that the port had given us our money's worth, and that there was more peace on the deep sea than in that uneasy harbour. In the light dawn air we allowed the tide to carry us against the east pier, and the things Vincent said about the place as he jabbed at the stonework with his boathook very nearly relieved my own feelings. Not quite, though; I have never been into Ramsgate since, although I have often anchored off the North Foreland for the night and found such peace and comfort as Ramsgate cannot give. As the harbour master at Weymouth once said to me when I was cursing the place in a north-east gale: 'You people come here and because it is called a harbour you think it's all right. The anchorage here in a north-east gale is off the White Nore.' That was sound advice.

The light west wind blew us past the West Hinder and into Ostend just as they were lighting up. The dock gates were not open, and we tied up outside them until the tide had done its share. When the gates were on the point of opening, three hefty shore loafers jumped on our deck and proceeded to take charge, to the amusement of a coasting schooner, the *Damaris* of Goole, which was going in ahead of us. I ordered them off the deck but they refused to go, and I was in some doubt whether they were not acting under the orders of the harbour authorities as my French and their Flemish did not take me very far. After we were tied up in the dock, outside the schooner which was up against the quay, they demanded ten francs apiece for their services, which had consisted of getting in the way. This was too much for my well-known British phlegm, so Vincent and I manhandled them on board the schooner, whose mate did the rest in a thoroughgoing manner for which I have loved him ever since. It was a good thing for them that he was unable to get within reach of the submarine crew who sank his ship and drowned the crew during the war. He told me that the loafers were a well-known gang of ruffians, and that the harbour master would be grateful if I handed them over to him. Later that gentleman said he had seen the rumpus from the quay, and was going to send us help to get rid of them but, from what he could see, we were well able to manage our own troubles without assistance from him.

We stayed in Ostend for three days. It is a dull place unless your taste runs to casinos and overdressed women. Then, late at night, we went into the tidal harbour and the next morning entered the lock opening into the canal for Bruges. This canal rather worried me as it had just over five feet of water and, if there were any bumps in it, we were bound to stick. There was a light fair wind so we did not have to get out and tow, the only alternative, and evening saw us approaching Bruges along a straight stretch of the canal. With the sun lighting up the houses and the belfry tower it was a beautiful sight. We had been interested coming along the canal to meet huge barges towed by teams of three or four women, who had solved the problem of doing three things at once and doing them all well: towing, knitting and gossiping. The male members of the crews lolled in the stern and steered.

Bruges was a never-failing source of delight. With the local equivalent of a shilling, a franc, Vincent and I used to go up to the square in the evening, sit on one of the chairs belonging to the outdoor café and listen to the carillon played at nine from the belfry tower. When that was over the population seemed to go to bed, and the cafés and streets were deserted. In absolute silence we made our way back to the canal where our topmast nestled among the branches of the trees growing on the bank. The cathedral, the museums, and the wonderful lace curtains on the windows of even the poorest houses are my chief memories of Bruges.

The canal between Bruges and Ghent was rumoured to have less than the requisite five feet, and I had a yarn with a man who ran a regular motor towage service to Ghent as to whether it was possible for me to go through this canal. If not I should have to go down the canal to Zeebrugge and enter Holland at Flushing. He told me that although the canal was supposed to have at least five feet there were many places where accumulations of soft mud had decreased the depth, and that it would be impossible for me to sail or mantow the yacht past these places. He strongly advised me to hang on to the last of a string of barges he was sending to Ghent. His tug could easily drag me through the soft muddy patches. When I asked rather doubtfully how much this would cost he refused to make any charge at all but said, quite reasonably, that it might make things easier for me if I gave a tip to his tugmaster. I did not know how much this exalted official might consider adequate remuneration, but my friend said that ten francs would brand me as generous but not foolish. So for eight shillings and four pence I was towed thirty-eight miles to Ghent, and the way the tow-rope on occasion became as taut as a bar of iron proved, beyond cavil, that I could not have done it without assistance.

The scenery on the banks of the canal was not very interesting, but there was plenty of traffic to amuse us as we went along. It was on this stretch, as we approached Ghent, that we first met the huge barges in tow of powerful tugs steered by a horizontal wheel, whose diameter was the same as the beam of the barge, and worked by a couple of men walking round a circular platform with their chests against the spokes. The bargees carried their families with them living in beautifully kept deckhouses aft. Front door disputes were avoided by the provision of separate entrances for the various families. The toddlers were secured by ropes tied round their waists of such a length that if a child fell overboard he would hang suspended clear of the water. Of course, all the barges carried schipperkes, and the chief duty of these dogs seemed to be telling tales when the children were likely to be naughty. Some of the barges carried as much as 300 tons, and later in the big canals and estuaries we were to meet barges from the Rhine districts capable of carrying over 1000 tons. This barge traffic does mean cheap transport.

The barge immediately ahead of us during the towage was a small one of about 50 tons capacity, the crew consisting of one man and his wife. The toddler of three could hardly yet be considered an effective member of the ship's company. During the whole of the tow, which lasted for twelve hours, the man was busily employed in getting a shine on his ship, and our one conversation was when he waved a brush and a tin can in the air and shouted, '*Englische Vernisse! Bon!*' I replied '*Tres bon*', and there our intelligibility, one to the other, ended. But the toddler made several desperate efforts to get on board the yacht when we came close together in the locks at Ghent, and was played like a salmon by the mother as soon as there was any risk attached to its movements.

After being shifted about a lot, and generally given the impression that nobody quite knew what to do with us, we were tied up alongside a Belgian steam yacht, whose skipper, in perfect English, spent a lot of his owner's time in reflecting how much wealthier than I he must be, bringing forward many obvious and unnecessary arguments to prove his point, which I had not the least intention of disputing. The result was to implant in my mind a deadly hatred for the said owner, mixed with a truly British contempt for a man who was so lost to all sense of decency and the eternal fitness of things as to have a nosegay of artificial flowers on his deck saloon table. When I did meet the owner, and accepted his invitation to come on board for a yarn, I found him a man after my own heart who regretted deeply that the increasing cares of his business and the nature of his cruising grounds made it essential that he should own a power-driven vessel if he were to go to sea at all. He apologized for the artificial flowers with a grin, saying that his skipper was responsible for them, and he did not like to order their removal for fear of offending his sus-ceptibilities. The Anglo-Belgian entente was sealed in some excellent Scotch. We saw very little of Ghent itself as we were not able to go ashore except late in the evening, and found that if we did not return to the dock with the last tram at nine we would have to walk the long distance. We caught that tram, and by that time the town had gone to bed. The early habits of all the places we visited in Belgium and Holland were very marked.

By pushing, pulling and shoving, and also by surreptitiously hanging on to the sterns of towed barges, we managed to enter the deep sea canal that connects Ghent with the West Schelde. This was very wide and deep, and we could easily have sailed along it, but there is no known method of sailing a yacht when there is no wind. Seeing our predicament a big English steamer going down the canal tried to give us a tow but the rope they threw us fell short, and as the captain dare not go astern in the canal he had perforce to leave us.

Somehow or other we managed to struggle by the evening to Sas van Gent on the Dutch frontier, where some Dutch customs officers were fishing from a pier. They at once left off their recreation to attend to business, and I won-dered what kind of examination they would give me. Seizing hold of my lines they towed me round the end of the pier into a little backwater where, they told me, I would be quite safe from disturbance by the night traffic in the ca-nal, and then politely hoped that I would enjoy my stay in Holland. As they made no further movement and I wanted to get the clearance over I asked whether they were coming on board. The answer was that I was already clear and free to go ashore for a walk if I wished. If I meant to leave very early in the morning the papers would be brought to me at once, but if I were in no hurry they would return to their fishing, as this was the time the fish were biting. When the clearance did come I asked the officer whether he wished to search the ship. The answer gave me a glow of pride. 'It is never neces-sary to examine yachts belonging to English gentlemen.' They had a different outlook from the two boarding-house keepers who discussed their difficulties on a seat beside me on the front at Southsea. One summed it up in the biting statement: 'You see the trouble is that you can't get good prices for rooms in Southsea because there aren't any gentry here. There's nothing but naval and military officers.'

A strong westerly wind the next morning blew us down to Terneuzen where we were locked on to the broad bosom of the Schelde for a smart turn to windward on an ebbing tide to Flushing. There was plenty of water flying about, and the red duster on our mizen mast was well frayed before we arrived. I suppose we must have been an inspiriting sight—I know we were thoroughly enjoying our first sail after the canals—since the crew of an English steamer passing up the river to Antwerp lined their fo'c'sle head and cheered us, while the captain raised his gold-laced cap. Certainly we were the only sailing craft in the river that day, and we were making short miles of it in spite of the adverse wind.

We entered Flushing harbour and, try our utmost, we could not sail *Dorothy* into the lock which gave access to the Walcheren canal. Strong eddying flaws spun us round and round just when we were within an ace of success. Finally, Vincent ran away a line in the dinghy and we were ignominiously hauled in by the nose. When I apologized to the harbour master for the delay our antics had caused, he confessed he had enjoyed our efforts and had been wondering if he were going to see, for the first time, a yacht sail into the lock under the prevailing conditions. Just inside the lock we tied up to the canal bank and wandered off to see the attractions of Flushing. I believe I am not the only one who has failed to find them. But there was something to be said for the outlook when we stood on the sea wall and gazed over the storm-tossed water towards the Wielingen channel, and marked the masses of broken water and a couple of tall sailing ships anchored on the bank opposite the entrance to the harbour.

Next day was Thursday, and we had timed our arrival so that we could slip along the canal and be in Middelbourg on that day. Everyone had told us the same thing: 'Whatever you see or miss seeing in Holland be sure not to miss the Thursday market in Middelbourg.' I can only, from the bottom of my heart, repeat that advice. There are parts of Holland where the scenery, the people, and their costumes are commercialized to an extent only equalled by the Pyramids. But Middelbourg is the real thing and the visitor is not looked upon as the proverbial fool with money. They are there to do their business just as their ancestors have done for hundreds of years, and they are gravely courteous to the interloper in all their gestures. To you they are quaint, and to them you are probably ludicrous, but you are more likely to betray your impression than they are. The pride they betray in their children is not one of the least fascinating of their many attractive characteristics.

The children deserve this pride. I have heard many complaints of the behaviour of the children towards visiting yachts but for my own part I have never had any of these unpleasant experiences; but then I liked the children and always tried to make friends with them and usually invited them on board. The tendency of a certain type of visitor is to look upon a departure from the recognized standards of their own country as an excuse for behaving as if the 'natives' were occupants of a zoo specially trotted out for their delectation. Amongst the young friends I made in Holland a typical one was the son of the harbour master in Flushing, a lad of thirteen. His first enquiry was whether I knew Mr Arthur Briscoe. Luckily I could claim the friendship of that distinguished marine artist, and after that he was a frequent visitor. He was very anxious to improve his English which was quite fluent, and perhaps he was not averse to an opportunity for practice, but if he were a fair sample of the children of his class, there are many of his age in England who have much to learn from him.

The market day over we went on to Veere, and as there was a light head wind Vincent and I took turns along the towpath. We towed with a very light line from the masthead, the end of the line being made fast to the fore halliard. In this way obstructions on the bank were easily cleared. When you met a tow coming in the opposite direction one party dropped the line, which was then wound up by the man on board, who also sheered his ship towards the other side of the canal so as to leave plenty of room for passing. When they had passed, the dropping ship came in towards the towpath again, and the man on board threw the end of the towline to the man on the bank. He made it fast

Locking through

to the harness over his shoulders and the tow was resumed. Towing was very slow work—we found it impossible to get along any faster than three knots— but it was not hard work once you had got the boat moving. It seemed rather curious that all tows proceeded at the same rate no matter whether they were heavily laden barges or smart yachts.

As the day faded we went alongside the staging on the port hand close to the lock at Veere. Supper and a bed were strongly indicated.

Early next morning I was wakened by a soft musical voice which repeated with monotonous persistence: 'Want you brood? Want you melk? Want you botther? Want you egg?' I looked out and, on the jetty alongside which we were lying, an elderly Dutchman, looking for all the world like a picture postcard, was standing and reiterating his plaint. His left arm was threaded through the handle of an enormous marketing basket covered with a clean white cloth, while his right hand gave courage and support to a tiny maiden who was viewing with apprehension her grandfather's efforts at rousing the sleeping British lion. I was in need of all he had for sale, but most of all I wanted to make the acquaintanceship of his charming companion. I found that even at the mature age of three she had, like the rest of her sex, a shrewd idea of the cash value of her favours. For the exorbitant sum of one dubbeltje she was willing to allow a not too long handclasp, and that was as far as my finances allowed our flirtation to get. She was the exact replica of her mother whom I saw with her later in the town, but the little flirt was evidently satisfied that I was a poor man because she refused me the privilege of recognition.

Veere is an ancient city with a wonderful cathedral, a Stadhuis, and a fishing port, but the glory has departed long ago and it lies in a backwater only saved from oblivion by the proximity of the Walcheren canal which at this point enters the estuary of the East Schelde. Yet of all the towns of Holland which I have visited at various times it always remains the most attractive, from its history, its deserted public buildings, and its air of sleepy abstraction from the turmoil of life. We stayed here for three days this time, as strong head winds and an unwillingness to turn to windward through the Zandcreek accentuated the comfort and idleness of the canal jetty.

It was as well we stayed, as a letter from Chatham arrived and ordered my return within a week. If we were to see any more of Holland we would have to scamper. So the next morning we locked out of the canal and sailed for all we were worth up the Zandcreek into the Englische Vaarwater, and made a desperate effort at getting to Dordrecht but a failing wind and an adverse tide compelled us to put in to Zujpe. The next morning there was a strong head wind for Dordrecht but a fair wind back and I dare not waste it, so we turned round and sailed into the lock of the canal to Goes. I knew there was not sufficient water in the canal to allow me to sail the three miles to the town so I asked the harbour master where I could lie inside the lock. For the first time I found an official who could not speak fluent English. He made no reply but walked away, leaving me rather puzzled what to do as ours was only one of several vessels in the lock, and we had to get out of the way of the others to allow them to proceed up the canal. In a short time a small girl was addressing me in precise and very perfect English. 'My father is the harbour master and he is anxious to know what it is you want him to do.' The father had joined her and was gazing with doting admiration at the small mouth which could deal with the foreigner in such a masterly fashion. There was a short conversation between them, the result of which was that I was comfortably stowed away in a corner out of the way of traffic. After I was tied up I went to look for the interpreter and thanked her for coming to the rescue. I suggested that she must have visited England to be able to speak the language so well, but she said she had been taught all the English she knew in the village school. She volunteered the information that she was teaching father but he was very slow and shy.

I walked the three miles into the town of Goes, but excepting the church there was nothing of interest. The day was a Monday and the verger was sweeping out the church. The sweepings were chiefly cigar butts, and he explained that when the sermon was dull the burgher eased the tedium with a cigar. His surprise at my astonishment and my surprise at his explanation were about equal. There is much to be said for the custom. My Dutch money had run out and I was recommended to try the tobacconist, who not only gave me a very good exchange rate but threw in as discount several miniature cacti in earthenware pots. Cultivation of these cacti was a favourite hobby in Holland but the ones presented to me did not take kindly to a seafaring life.

When it was time to leave the following morning, there was a strong wind blowing up the narrow gut leading to the lock, and it was impossible to beat down. We made several efforts but ran aground every time as there was no room to get way on the ship. Finally, half a dozen men took a towline and ran me down the gut at such a pace that we got clear. In less than an hour we were through the lock at Veere and sailing fast along the Walcheren canal towards Flushing. The bridge at Middelbourg opened in record time when they saw us coming, but even then we rasped the bridge with our forestay as we pushed it in front of us. The harbour master's son came down to see us at once, but he was very poor comfort for the start we meant to make at four o'clock next morning. 'There is a strong wind for you,' he repeated, at every interval in the conversation. There was one good thing about it, it was a fair wind and, with my leave nearly up, that was a gift horse not to be looked in the mouth.

At four o'clock, when we locked out, the wind had not taken off any. In spite of the early hour the boy had come to see us off, and he shivered on top of the quay as we passed into the harbour and, hanging on to a shore line, got the canvas up. It was a strong wind and we were making the passage under three reefs and a storm jib, but we tore across the North Sea like a donkey with a thistle under its tail, and at 7 p.m. when the North Foreland was abeam it was blowing harder than ever. I chose the Overland passage as I wanted to get in before dark, but it was early dark that night, and we had some hectic moments looking out for the unlit Cant buoys as we entered the Medway. However, luck stayed with us, and by ten the anchor was down and the canvas stowed, in Queenborough. We had taken well under eighteen hours to do the 110 miles; and the last thirty, with a strong flood under us, had been done in less than three hours. This is the fastest passage I have ever done in a small yacht under canvas. Next day we heard of another peril of the sea which, luckily, we had not thought of or it would have scared us stiff. Three barges had sunk on the edge of the Cant while trying to make the Medway the previous afternoon. If ever I were mixed up in the gear of a sunken barge in a gale of wind I am sure the experience would drive me to golf or bridge as an amusement.

In all my forty years of cruising this was the only occasion when I had any dispute with the Customs. A youth, who must have been new to the station at Queenborough, came on board in response to the ensign flying at my masthead. He took it upon himself to rate me soundly for not complying with the port regulations, in failing to anchor or heave-to outside the harbour on the Cant Edge until he was able to come out and clear me. I told him that he evidently knew nothing about the sea, and that I would not have hove-to last night on the Cant Edge for anybody or anything on this earth. He promised to report me to higher authorities in Chatham, and I presume he must have done so for a few days later I received a graceful apology for the ill-judged zeal of a junior officer.

XI

The Bristol Channel

I T WAS THE MONTH OF FEBRUARY when I turned over my duties in Chatham to my relief and went up to the Admiralty to find out what was to become of me. There I learned that I was to be appointed to a Hospital ship, but the ship was refitting at Malta and was not expected in England for six weeks. In the meantime I would be placed on half pay. On protesting against this period of penury being forced upon me, I was lent to the Barracks as supernumerary and ordered to report myself in accordance. When I turned up, the senior medical officer was not at all gratified by this distinguished addition to his staff. He very tactfully suggested that I was a nuisance as my seniority made it difficult for him to employ me without interfering with his normal arrangements, and he did not feel inclined to upset his routine in order to keep me out of mischief for so short a period as six weeks. His solution of the problem was that the less he saw of me the better he would like me, and that the best thing I could do was to go on leave and keep him informed of my address in case my services might be required, a contingency of which he saw little prospect. For the first time in my life I had six weeks' leave in my pocket and no programme to fill up every minute of it.

For some years I had been deeply interested in Bristol Channel pilot boats and the possibility of their adaptation for yachting purposes. By all accounts they were wonderful seaboats, cheap to build and maintain, and a bigger ship than anything I had been accustomed to could be handled with only one man as crew. The last was an important consideration for me as my pay could not run to the wages of any more men. After donning my oldest yachting suit and stuffing plenty of warm underclothing and sea boots into a seaman's canvas bag, I looked the complete ruffian when I purchased a third-class ticket for a little village on the Avon not far from Bristol. The consensus of opinion was that this was the best place to see these boats, and in the back of my mind was the hope that I might have the chance of getting inside information usually denied to the lordly yachtsman before I decided to spend several hundred pounds, which I hadn't got but hoped I might be able to raise, in buying one of them. Above everything I wanted to make sure that they were really within the power of two men and, as I was an average yachtsman, experience would enable me to judge this point quite fairly. I could not afford to make a mistake and bite off something a great deal bigger than I was able to chew.

In due time and in pitch darkness I was deposited as the sole passenger at the village station. This place was the headquarters of a large fleet of pilot boats and there were two famous building yards nearby. When I tumbled out of my compartment and went to the luggage van to collect my bundle I was the only occupant of the platform excepting the porter, who came along and watched with polite interest the struggles of the guard and myself, but did not make any attempt at help. He still stood watching me after the train had gone, asked for my ticket, and after its delivery was strolling off when I called him back. To state the truth I was annoyed at his casual treatment and intended to rate him soundly, tell him to pick up my dunnage, and look for a cab. Luckily, before I made a fool of myself, I recognized that his treatment was an acknowledgement that my disguise was perfect. To him I was an ordinary seaman probably looking for a job and of no interest. So when he turned round all I said was:

'I'm a stranger in these parts. Could you tell me if there is any place where I can find decent lodgings?'

He thought for a bit, pushed back his uniform cap and scratched the exposed area while he eyed me doubtfully.

'Well, my missus sometimes takes in lodgers and I know she has an empty room just now, but whether she's willing to take any more on her hands we'll have to leave to her.'

There was no doubt left that his missus might be anything but grateful for his production of such a scallywag. I said we had better get along and find out what she thought about it, and he promised to take me to the house as soon as he had locked up the station as there were no more trains that night. I threw my bag across my shoulder in true sailor fashion and followed him out of the station when he was ready. The bag was heavy, and I was glad to think that railway employees were not likely to live far from their work as my proposed host had not the faintest intention of lending a hand. The walk was longer than I expected and, when I finally dropped the bag on his doorstep, the man of much experience remarked sympathetically:

'Very heavy them bags is and yours is bigger than most. Better leave it on the step until we hears what the missus has to say.' He pushed open the door and I followed him into the kitchen.

Our entry disturbed a pleasant little supper party seated at a table close to a roaring fire, which was a welcome sight on that bitter February night. At the end of the table nearest to us sat a buxom pleasant-faced woman, while on her right was a man about my own age opposite a girl of thirteen or so. The far end of the table was laid for the lord and master, and keeping hot on top of the range was something that smelt uncommonly good. With a 'Here's a sailor that wants to know if you will let him have a room, mother', the porter threw his cap on the dresser, and apparently washed his hands of the rest of the proceedings at the sink.

The lady addressed as 'mother' pushed her chair back, turned round and took stock of me with both hands on her knees. Evidently the scrutiny was not entirely satisfactory.

'How long were you thinking of staying?'

'I'm not quite sure. It depends on whether I can get a job.'

'What was your last job?'

'I had a Government job at Chatham but that's finished.'

'Do you expect me to keep you until you get a job, or can you keep yourself?'

'I can keep myself for a bit if it isn't too long.' 'Where have you come from to-day?' 'I've come straight from Chatham.'

'My! That's a long way! Sit down and have a cup of tea and I'll talk it over with my old man.'

They went into the lobby and I heard them talk it over. She said 'I'll take him', and he said 'All right, mother'. Then they came back and the lady resumed the cross-examination.

'Do you want a room to yourself or will you share? That'll be sixteen shillings a week by yourself or twelve shillings sharing.'

I expressed a preference for having a room to myself, and she suggested that I had better have a look at it, to which I agreed. She lit a candle and I followed her upstairs. I was shown into a bedroom beautifully clean and fresh although overloaded with furniture and crockery knick-knacks.

'This is a very nice room,' I said. 'I hope you will find me a good lodger.'

The lady was a little embarrassed. 'You won't mind me asking you, but we always keep ourselves clean. You know what I mean. Seafaring folks can't always help it.'

I knew what she was so delicately hinting at and reassured her. 'There's nothing like that about me, you're not allowed to go about like that in Government jobs.' I thought of my marine servant's face if he knew that I had been suspected of being verminous, and had difficulty in keeping from smiling. There was still a last point to discuss, and I had the wit to guess what it was before she had said two words.

'You're quite right, as you know nothing about me. I'll pay you a week in advance.' I handed her a golden sovereign and she carefully lifted up her skirt and from an enormous leather pouch slung round her waist produced the four shillings change. That was the end of the bargaining, and the next act was that I was seated at supper beside 'miss' and tucking into some of the best eggs and bacon I have ever tasted. Later, when we had become good friends, the porter confessed that his wife must have taken a sudden fancy to me as he had never expected she would have let me have the best bedroom, especially as he had been none too sure of me himself. 'Coming down in the dark like that and not offering me threepence to carry your bag! I thought there must be something queer about you, begging your pardon in a manner of speaking!' The last was a favourite phrase of his when he thought the compliments were getting a bit mixed.

Supper over, mother and daughter proceeded to the sink while we three men clustered round the fire and smoked. The young man was taking stock of me all the time and pumping me, with what object I could not determine, as to my experience at sea. He was visibly impressed when I admitted that I had been 'foreign'. 'That was in steamboats, I expect,' he said rather contemptuously. When I explained that I had been foreign in both steam and sail he dropped his suspicious manner, and told me that he was an apprentice pilot and first hand in a pilot cutter, but could not become qualified as a pilot until he had served a year in a foreign-going vessel. Just before we went to bed he said that the second hand in their cutter was sick and they were unable to go to sea. If I cared to put in for the job temporarily, he was sure the pilot would be glad to have me, as he was losing money by this delay. I asked what the pay would be, and was offered twenty-six shillings a week and my grub when at sea. There would be also my share in the pilotage which might amount to fifteen shillings a week or might be nothing. I said that I would think it over and should like to have a look at the ship before deciding but that I thought it would suit me. It was understood that, if I took the job, I would follow the custom of the pilot boatmen and pay the landlady six shillings a week as retainer for the room while I was at sea. That sounded reasonable enough, and—lest anyone should think that this was easy money for her—I was told to leave all my mending with her, and that she would do all the washing and mending necessary.

I went to bed well satisfied with myself. It was not much more than twelve hours since I had shed the conventional shackles of a naval officer, and here I was as good as engaged and earning enough to make me a self-respecting member of a seafaring community. I wondered how long it would be before I was discovered to be the fraud I really was and got the boot. Bill had told me that no seaman's discharges were required by the pilots so one source of exposure was removed.

Early the next morning after a jolly good breakfast my new friend and I went down to the creek, where about a score of pilot cutters were lying in mud berths at low water. It had been snowing during the night and there was a sharp frost. The deck of the cutter was covered with ice, and the first thing Bill did, after telling me to stay where I was, was to dive down the fo'c'sle hatch and reappear with a shovelful of ashes which he sprinkled over the deck. This made our footing safe enough but, accustomed as I was to the sacred purity of scrubbed teak, horrified me and drew a protest, much to Bill's amusement. 'These navy ways aren't much use here. The decks are painted with a mixture of tar and paraffin and won't take any harm.'

I had never been on board one of these vessels before, and this one which we were in was said to belong to the biggest and best class. She was fifty-three feet over all, forty-eight on the waterline, thirteen feet six inches beam, drew nine feet aft and three feet six inches forward. She was very heavily built and all the gear seemed to promise heavy working. I did not like the outline of her deck since it had the appearance of having been pinched between a gigantic finger and thumb just abaft the rigging, an ugly feature I have noticed in many working craft which have not been built to well designed lines. The deck arrangements were simple, and had been purposely reduced to the minimum so that there were no skylights and only two hatches. The after hatch led from the small deep cockpit into the saloon, the forrard entered the fo'c'sle on the port side of the midship line, so as to be clear of the bowsprit when it was run in. A few scattered deck lights allowed you to avoid collision below, but did not supply anything that could be called light. There was no ventilation except through the hatches and the fo'c'sle chimney, which pierced the deck abaft the bitts. As all these openings were bound to be closed in bad weather I could have forecasted with certainty the solid atmosphere I was destined to meet—and enjoy—on many future occasions. The bowsprit bitts were three enormous blocks of timber rising high above the stemhead and much stronger than was needed in order to support the crab windlass and bowsprit. Later when we were towed at fourteen knots astern of an ocean-going steamer I was to learn that they were barely enough for their job.

The deck was protected by bulwarks about sixteen inches high with opening doors amidships to allow the dinghy to be dragged on board. The rigging had been reduced to the minimum possible. There were no bowsprit shrouds, bobstay, or foretopmast stay, no runners, the triple shrouds being widely spread apart in lieu, no topmast shrouds or backstays. The main and peak halliards were led through leading blocks, in the covering board on each side, to bollards fitted on either side of the cockpit and within easy reach of the helmsman. The fore-sheet was a single part as far as the leading bulls eye, and thence was controlled by a powerful gun-tackle purchase, the standing block of which was made fast to the forrard of the two bollards at the side of the cockpit. There were no cross-trees at the hounds but an iron spur was fitted in their place for the all-round white light which was the only navigation light these ships carried. The mainsail, made of very heavy canvas and about 900 square feet in area, was laced along the foot to a wooden jackstay on the solid pitchpine boom which weighed just short of three hundredweight. The gaff, also very heavy, was almost the same length as the boom and the head of the sail squarer than is usual in yachts. Reefing was effected by the Appledore reefing gear with which I was unfamiliar although I had heard it warmly commended.

The mainsheet interested me most of all. This sheet was double-ended, the ends being made fast to the after bollards on each side of the well, and the purchase being made by means of two double blocks. Between the lower block and the main horse was an enormous spring buffer, and there was a similar buffer between the upper block and the boom. The pilots were in the habit of jibing their vessels all standing, under almost any conditions of wind and sea, and these buffers allowed this to be done without injury to the boom. The most common accident to which they were liable was the breaking of the boom when the sail was reefed, as the mere weight of wind would break the spar where the leach joined it, in the same way as a stick is snapped across the knee. The deck was free from encumbrances of any kind, and there were no rails or stanchions along the bulwarks. It struck me that this unprotected stretch of deck might well seem the loneliest place on God's earth when I left the security of the cockpit to do a job up forrard.

Going down a short steep ladder from the cockpit the compass was seen on a shelf under the sliding hatch in such a position that it was badly lit during the day and almost invisible at night, while it was in the worst possible position for taking bearings. Bill's remark that they didn't bother with the compass much was borne out by the marlinspike and spare shackle stowed in a handy shelf close beside it. At the bottom of the ladder was a passageway about eight feet long between storerooms, sailracks, and a small compartment furnished with a seat and a bucket. This was never used at sea, direct contact being then made with the sewage system in a primitive fashion. A double door with glass panels admitted to the saloon, a large room about ten feet long and with six feet width of floor space. On either side were box bunks entered by a small oval hole, the edges of the hole decorated with mahogany moulding. The bunk was very narrow and once inside you were as securely fixed as if you had been screwed down in a coffin, to which the bunk bore a strong resemblance. In front of the bunks were narrow settees, and between the bunks and the settees the ship's legs were stowed when not in use. Fixed against the after bulkhead and on either side of the door were two mahogany chests of drawers, and against the forrard bulkhead on the port side of the fo'c'sle doorway was the table, which was a fixed one and covered the water tank holding sixty gallons or more.

The fo'c'sle was similarly fitted, the table against the after bulkhead forming the cable locker, and having the same type of bunks and settees but without the mahogany trimmings. The main addition to the furniture was the cooking range, a small Hostess, secured to the bitts where they passed through the floor to be embedded in the keel. The ship was open right up to the stem but there was an unholy row if anyone ventured to hang as much as an oilskin forrard of the bitts. The pilots believed that the dryness of the ship at sea depended on keeping the ends light and the weights amidships. I am sure they were right.

I have described the ship at some length because since the war many of them have been 'converted' into yachts, and in the process all their best features have been altered until, except in hull appearance, they no more resemble pilot boats than any other old 'tore-out'. I speak feelingly because I, who ought to have known better, was fool enough to 'convert' two of them after the war as there was a shortage of yachts within the purchasing power of my gratuity. One of them was inspected by a pilot cutter hand in Brixham, and when I asked him what he thought about it his answer accorded with my own experience. 'Poor old *Freda*! You've spoiled a good seaboat but you've got a very fine houseboat.'

It was rather disappointing to find that the headroom below was only sufficient to let me stand up between the beams in the saloon, although it was a little better in the fo'c'sle. That was due to the bulky nature of her ballast which was all inside and consisted of scrap iron and steel punchings. The pilots disliked headroom as it meant heavy ballast concentrated low down and an uneasy ship in consequence. When considering these vessels it has to be remembered that the livelihood of their owners depended on their ability to keep the sea in any weather. They simply had to be on the spot when wanted, and it was only possible to do so if the ships were so easy at sea that even the wildest weather could not drive them in for shelter. That they fulfilled their functions admirably may be guessed when I say that I could find no record of one of those ships being lost through stress of weather. Losses, of course, there had been in plenty, but all of them had been due to collision, fire, or stranding. The power of the wind and sea alone had never overwhelmed one of them. Remember that we are speaking of the Bristol Channel in winter. One yachtsman I knew used to take off his hat and keep a moment's silence if anyone mentioned cruising in this area in his presence. The gesture was not meant as a joke.

Whilst I was nosing round and finding my way about, Bill was sweeping up the floor and tidying the cabins. He lit the stove—there was no method of heating the saloon—and after we had finished our respective occupations we sat down to talk things over. The questions I had asked and that I thought would betray my greenness had seemed to him just the intelligent desire for information that any man ought to show before taking on a new billet. When he had answered a whole string of queries he asked me whether I would join up at once, as the pilot was anxious to get away the next day to meet a big ship which was shortly due and would be worth a lot of money to all of us. If he could report that he had got a second hand he would be able to provision ship at once. There was only one pilot in this ship instead of the usual two, and I suggested that she would prove heavy working for only three hands. At this Bill threw back his head and roared with laughter. 'The pilots don't help in the work of them ships. They're real gents. You and I will have to do all the work by ourselves, but we can manage it easy. I could do it by myself, only a man must get some sleep sometime when he may be a week at sea.'

I looked at his big powerful frame and could well believe him, but I was a much smaller man though tough enough and in good fettle. The next thing to do was to interview the pilot and get his approval. He was a big burly man with a secret sorrow which I was able to do something to assuage. He had been chosen as the pilot of the Royal Yacht when she came to Avonmouth to open the new docks, and when entering the lock she had rubbed her gang-way ladder against the side of the lock and damaged it, so that it could not be used for the disembarkation of the royal party. He told me this when he learned that I had been in a government job, and added that he had never felt so ashamed in his life, and imagined all sorts of contempt had been showered on him by the naval officers who had been witnesses of the mishap. I thought of the times I had seen a ladder smashed by picket boats coming alongside, and said: 'I don't suppose they ever thought anything about it except to curse somebody for not having a fender handy.' This was a new idea to the old man and, coming as it did from one who claimed to know the service attitude, eased a load which he admitted he had been carrying for years. Incidentally, it also convinced him that I was the very man he wanted as temporary second hand, and allowed us to start on good terms. I wondered how long it would be before he found the very moderate value of my opinion on nautical affairs. It was arranged that Bill and I were to take the ship to Portishead the next day and lie in a mud berth. He was to join us in the evening, and we would get to sea on the early morning tide.

We filled in the afternoon and evening after the fashion of young men all over the world, that is to say we talked a little, smoked a good deal, ate more than was necessary, and spent most of the dark hours in a little local institute where there was a reading room and a very good billiard table. Although a fairly good billiard player, judged by mess room standards, I preferred to yarn with the seamen who were constantly coming and going. Almost without exception they were pilot-boat men or had some connexion with the calling and were the finest, clean-living types of men I have ever met. There was a comradeship and good feeling extended to the stranger which could only have been equalled in a wardroom mess. Their talk was all of the sea and ships, and in no way defaced by the bad language and doubtful stories that too often pass for wit in some nautical circles. I am always proud to remember that they welcomed me as one of themselves, and if ever I should be in mortal peril from the sea I could ask and hope for no better shipmates than these pilot-boat men from the Bristol Channel.

Late that night after being delightfully fussed over and stuffed by our landlady we went on board as it was necessary to be under way before dawn. It must have been desperately cold during the dark hours but, tucked away in the fo'c'sle bunks, and with the stove going full blast, we were as snug as the proverbial bugs, of which pest I was relieved to find no trace. There were snow and ice on the deck when we turned out under a dark blue frosty sky, and dawn was still in the future as we slipped our moorings and reached the fairway of the Avon. There was hardly a breath of wind, and we got the canvas on her easily enough although the halliards and sails were frozen stiff. There was nothing to do until we got to Portishead so Bill went to stir the fire and get breakfast ready while I did my best to obey his injunction to keep her in the middle of the river. The breakfast was cooked, eaten and cleared up before we edged out of the tide and picked up our berth on top of a mudbank opposite the village. The pilot joined in the evening and told us he had arranged with a friendly steamer to be towed as far as Lundy. I thought this was good news as the wind was too light to get us anywhere, but for some reason Bill did not seem quite so pleased. When I asked him why, he told me I'd very soon find out.

Dawn found us at the mouth of the river waiting for the steamer from Bristol, and soon she hove in sight and took our line. Before we had been astern of her for five minutes I knew exactly what Bill meant. I was steering and the steamer worked up to fourteen knots in next to no time. Luckily it was a flat calm, but the speed at which we were towed brought a constant shower of spray over the fo'c'sle head and slap into my face where I stood in the cockpit. The bite of the icy spray was painful misery. I dodged it as best I could by ducking behind the companion, but with little success as the ship was very hard to steer, and I was afraid of pulling the bitts out of her if she were allowed to sheer about. In that trip to Lundy I learned to appreciate and be grateful for those enormous bitts. Bill and I found that an hour at the tiller was as much as either of us could stand, and we spent our watch below in front of the stove warming up for the next effort. That five-hour tow for long stood out as my most miserable experience at sea.

All things come to an end, and it was with unfeigned thankfulness we coiled in the tow-rope and hoisted the canvas midway between Lundy and Ilfracombe. There was a light westerly wind, and for the next twenty-four hours the ebb carried us towards Hartland and the flood towards the Bull. There were literally dozens of pilot boats all round from Barry, Cardiff, Pill, Swansea, and Newport, and there was a constant interchange of greetings as we passed one another or a ship slowed down to pick up or discharge her pilot. There did not seem to be any method in the allocation of jobs. The incoming steamer bore down on the pilot cutter whose lettering on her mainsail indicated that she belonged to the desired port, and hailed for a pilot. If one were available he went on board, if not the steamer went on to the next cutter. Occasionally the captain of the steamer asked for a special pilot, and if the cutter were anywhere handy the captain was allowed his choice, but the steamer could not afford to wait, and if he could not easily get the pilot he wanted the captain would take any one who offered. At night time the steamer could not see the markings on the sail, and then the pilot cutter burned the appropriate flares or the steamer hailed for information as she passed. The arrangement seems rather primitive but it worked all right and, although there was plenty of rivalry, there was no trace of ill-feeling and no jealousy was shown when a captain asked for his favourite pilot. Probably the reason for this comradeship

Britannia
The final stage in the development of the Bristol Channel Pilot Cutter
Note the overhang forward

was to be found in the fact that there was no economic drive as all the men were earning good money.

The pilot in our boat was exceptional, but he confessed to earning over a thousand a year, and many of the other men were not far behind him. Of course it can be readily understood that the fees for a large ship of deep draught were much higher than those for a smaller ship. We were waiting for a very large ship whose captain had warned the pilot that he expected to be off Lundy at a certain time, and it was well worth his while to let the small fry go past. Most of the cutters carried two pilots and either picked up or dropped their pilots as required. When both pilots had been placed on homeward bound ships the cutter went back to her home port to pick them up, and provision and water. If the pilots were expected to come back in an outward bounder the cutter went into Ilfracombe to provision and water there. The stay in port rarely exceeded four days unless the cutter were due for a refit, and the time on station might be anything but was usually ten days to a fortnight. The new steamer pilot service in which the pilot carries out his duties according to a roster may be more efficient, but it is responsible for an enormous amount of unemployment and the virtual extinction of the finest body of seamen in the world whose services can ill be spared.

I soon tumbled to the routine on board. Bill and I kept watch and watch, the hand turning out getting a meal ready and consuming it before relieving the deck. After my first effort at cooking the dinner Bill decided that it had better be prepared by himself if we were to remain friends. We saw very little of the pilot, who took no part in the deck work except to take the tiller, but who grumbled like a wardroom mess at the meals we placed in front of him with unfailing regularity. He insisted on drinking huge quantities of camomile tea, which we prepared for him, and it was not long before I was certain that he was suffering from a gastric ulcer, of which he was fond of telling me the symptoms without guessing that his second hand was making a medical diagnosis. Like many people of his class he would not seek medical advice although relief, if not complete cure, of his symptoms would have been easy.

It was a fixed rule, from which there was no departure during the time I was on board, that the watch below must never be disturbed. If there was anything to be done that required both hands it was left until the change of the watch. A two-handed job only took place once, and then it was my fault, more due to ignorance than lack of strength. As far as the hoisting of the canvas was concerned there was no great difficulty, but I was doubtful whether the anchor and cable were within the powers of one man assisted by the clumsy crab winch. The anchor annoyed me as it was a bad shape, and I was sure it had no more holding power than that conferred by its excessive weight. Bill laughed at my fears, and said that it was a very rare thing for the cutters to anchor except for a short time waiting for the tide in order to enter the inner harbour at Ilfracombe. So far I had not seen anything like bad weather, and was not fated to do so this first trip. The second morning after leaving the Avon we put the pilot on board the expected vessel, and with a light fair wind sailed back to our moorings. On arrival we were told that we need not put to sea for a couple of days, when we would return to our station off Lundy and take the pilot off an outward bound ship. Except for the cold which had been intense the whole trip had been more like a summer cruise. I had added nothing to my knowledge of the Channel, and had seen nothing of its wilder moods which have caused the writer of one book of sailing directions to say: 'Except in settled summer weather a craft unable to keep the sea should be considered unsafe for use in the Bristol Channel if far from an accessible harbour, on account of the rapidity with which the sea may get up, and it should be clearly realized that for this reason, making a passage in, say, a five-ton yacht, is quite a different proposition to doing the same thing in the English Channel or North Sea.'

On our second departure it was early in the forenoon when we swung into the river to catch all the ebb possible to help us in the long trip, which this time was to be made under canvas. Remembering the tow we had last time I was not sorry. The day was mild for the season and the sky overcast, and this combination allowed Bill to smell bad weather coming from the west, although when we started there was barely enough breeze to let us stem the tide, which had not quite finished running up. Once it did turn it gave me some idea of its fearful velocity as we whizzed past Avonmouth and entered the estuary of the Severn. There the wind was a little stronger, and we were soon sailing fast against a nasty choppy sea which would have made the casting off of a tow compulsory if we had been given one. Bill was glad of the breeze as he was anxious to get clear of the English and Welsh grounds and all the rest of the shoal water in the upper part of the estuary before dark. I was thoroughly enjoying myself as we tacked to windward in the first good sail I had had for nearly six months.

During the first dog watch, which I was keeping, I left the ship to herself and went below to get the sidelights but was told by Bill to hoist the pilot lamp instead. My answer was that we were not on our station and ought to have the side lights, but he insisted that I need not worry as none of the pilot cutters ever put up sidelights, and he was doubtful if half of them had their lights on board. There was no help for it so I hoisted the light at the masthead. Although its message was deceptive it proved a much better warning to steamers in our vicinity than any side lights in a small ship could have been. All the many ships passing up and down the channel gave us a wide berth and removed one very real cause for anxiety that had been worrying me ever since darkness had fallen.

During the second dog, which I spent below, it seemed to me that it was time I knew something about the waters in which I was supposed to be competent to take charge of a ship, but Bill had no gift for imparting information and I found, to my dismay, that there was not a single book of sailing directions nor a chart of any kind on board. Bill said there was a book of sailing directions somewhere but, when found after much searching, it proved to be an ancient copy of King's *Channel Pilot* and useless for my needs. There was a current copy of Brown's *Nautical Almanac*, that *vade mecum* of all coastwise sailors, but beyond the list of lights and a few courses and distances it did not help much. Bill was amused at my thirst for information and offered to tell me anything I wanted to know. After my threatening to come down and shake him up every time I was in difficulty during my watch, he promised that during the first watch he would give me a course that would keep me out of trouble and allow him his fair whack of sleep. He was, like all the other pilot men, a great sleeper, and had the enviable gift of being able to drop off for any odd moments that might be convenient. On the other hand he could keep awake for prolonged periods without his physical powers or his judgment being affected.

Down below in the fo'c'sle it was very snug that cold evening. The stove was burning brightly and, thanks to the forehatch being closed, the thick two-inch deck and planking, and the absence of skylights and ventilators, there was absolute silence, and the motion of the ship was easy and comfortable. As all comfort is relative, the enjoyment of my present condition was enhanced by the thought of Bill on deck and the remembrance that we would shortly change our respective occupations.

There is one essential virtue in a watchkeeper, lacking which all other good qualities are but sounding brass and tinkling cymbals, and that essential virtue is a smart relief. So at a quarter to the hour, after a mug of hot cocoa and some bread and butter, I got ready for my watch. Swathed up in a manner that would have satisfied even my mother I stepped into the well as the minute hand of the saloon clock marked the hour of eight. Bill was expecting me, and as soon as I spoke said, 'It's breezing up a bit. You take her and shake her up and I'll get the topsail off and shift to a smaller jib.' I don't think he took more than ten minutes over these two jobs for which he had evidently been preparing. He threw the wet sails on the racks in the alleyway, stripped off his oilskins and sea boots and left me with the comforting assurance, 'It's going to blow hard. Call me if you want anything.'

He hadn't been gone for half an hour before I wanted to call him like anything. The night was pitch dark and it was blowing and raining. I had not the faintest idea where we were or what course I ought to steer; in the scurry of taking the canvas off he had forgotten to give me any instructions. The ship was on the port tack, and I thought I could make out the loom of the land and shore lights to the southward, and there was something astern of me that might be Breaksea lightship, but I could not get its period in the rain squalls. I remembered that Bill had promised to leave me in such a position that I need have nothing to be anxious about for some hours so I supposed that he meant me to keep going on this tack. The compass suggested that we were heading north-west, but I trusted it not at all. Away in the north I caught a glimpse of the reflections in the sky of the Welsh coast towns, and this confirmed my idea that the ship was on the right tack.

In a little I settled down and took the opportunity of studying the behaviour of the vessel. So far everything was quite pleasant, the sea was long and easy and she was taking the waves nicely, an occasional biff on the weather bow and a shower of spray telling me in no uncertain language that it was up to me to see that she did not get any more than she could stand. So I eased her away or luffed, whichever I thought was best, when I saw a threatening curler coming up on my weather bow, and had no great difficulty in keeping her dry. By this means too I kept her from going too fast through the water. My reason for this was that the estuary is none too wide hereabouts, and I did not know how long I could carry on on this tack. In fact I was a hopelessly incompetent person to have sole charge of a vessel on a night like this, and I was playing for safety for all I was worth. When the tide turned as it would before my watch was up and we had wind against tide I guessed that things would not be so easy, but for the present I was thoroughly enjoying the sailing, the mad swoop to the top of a wave, the second we hung on the crest, the shower of spray on the fore deck, and then the slither sideways into the hollow, while for a fleeting moment the breaking wave made darkness visible. The ship was very easy on her helm, and it was not long before I discovered that, as long as I gave her a helping hand now and then, she was perfectly capable of looking after herself the rest of the time. Every sailing man will know what I mean by saying that I felt that the boat and I understood one another, and that we were good friends doing a rotten job together, but not getting in one another's way and not treading on each other's corns.

Towards the end of the watch we were getting across to the Welsh shore, and in the track of ships from Newport and Barry, and as I had no chart to guide me I began to think it was time to go about. The tide was just on the turn and the wind steadily increasing in force and, although the ship was not yet pressed, any great increase in the wind would entail some reduction of canvas. I watched my chance and got her round all right although she gave me an unhappy moment when she hung in stays while I was securing the jib sheets, which I was lucky enough to do at the precise second when a baby could have done it. After flapping doubtfully, the staysail was taken aback and soon forced her head round and then came the struggle to sheet the sail home. Thanks to the powerful tackle I managed it after shaking her up in the wind, and then I put up the helm and we crashed away on the starboard tack while I watched with interest, not unmixed with alarm, the sudden alteration in the character of the seas as the full force of the ebb met the increasing wind. The waves had lost all their easy roundness and become short and steep with breakers well forward of the crests. In spite of my nursing one of the crests caught her fairly on the bluff of the bow, and for a moment the whole ship disappeared in a cloud of spray, while far too much solid water came rushing aft and broke over the coaming into the cockpit. Luckily I had shipped the two lower fashion boards so that only a squirt went below, but I found that the self-draining scuppers acted very slowly, and I wondered what would happen if she were hit by a sea while still carrying a ton of water in her cockpit. A second blow, though not so severe, convinced me, if any conviction were necessary, that I was carrying too much canvas, and that the sooner it was reduced the happier I would feel.

Now happened the incident that gave me for the rest of my time in the cutter the reputation of being the most daredevil carrier-on that had ever served in those ships. I had looked forward to, some time or other, getting instruction in handling the Appledore reefing gear, but there had been no weather to compel its use, and I had only the haziest idea of how it worked. I had been warned in casual conversation that an improperly reefed sail was one of the commonest causes of a smashed boom, and touch one of those bar-taut straining ropes I would not until somebody who knew more about it than I did was present. Further, I was not going at this early stage of my career to risk being thought a disturber of the watch, so as far as I could see there was nothing to be done until the watch was called, and in the meantime I must nurse her through as best I could. I managed it, but the first thing Bill said when I called him was, 'My! It's blowing hard! Have you reefed her?' I summoned up all the casual coolness I was capable of in my reply. 'No, I haven't reefed. It's hardly bad enough for that yet if you want to get on.' Bill jumped as there was a staggering blow on our side and a cataract of water descended with a smash on the deck. 'Hark at him! Not blowing hard enough to reef! What do you think you're sailing? A line of battle ship?' He hurriedly donned his oilies and we went to the cockpit together where he remarked, 'Gawd!' as he looked around. Then, 'How in all the world did you get her round by yourself in this weather?' 'That was quite easy. She came round like a bird.' My answer seemed to incense him, and he threw the main halliard off the port forward bollard and eased down the throat of the sail for about two feet. Then he went forward, slacked away the single topping lift, and with the winch handle in the reefing gear, wound the boom a complete turn. He shouted to me to slack away the halliard handsomely so as to keep a taut luff as he rolled. The worm gear was very powerful, and he had not the least difficulty in winding up the four rolls he considered necessary, although the sail was soaking wet and as hard as a sheet of iron from the pressure of the wind.

He did not touch the peak halliard at all, and this was a very important point in using this type of reefing gear, since, if you take the weight of the boom on the topping lift and slack away the peak as in point reefing, the leach of the sail will not wind evenly round the boom, and you will have a slovenly reef which is likely to tear the sail. I have often been told, by disgruntled owners, of difficulties they have experienced with roller reefing, and all sorts of absurd suggestions have been made that a specially cut sail was necessary in order to get satisfactory results. I speak advisedly when I say that any difficulties with this gear are due to the user not knowing the correct method of handling the sail when the reef is being taken in. Since those far-off days I have used this gear for twenty years and have never had the least cause for complaint, although in two ships I have fitted Appledore reefing gear without making any alteration in the mainsails, which were originally fitted for pennant and point reefing. It was chiefly due to this gear that these large sailing vessels could be handled by a small crew, and it is nonsense to imagine that the boatmen would have tolerated a defective fitting when their lives and livelihood depended on it.

When Bill had finished with the mainsail he came and sat in the well but did not offer to take the helm, which I expected him to do, so that I could go below. After a little he said. 'I think we would be better without that jib.' I wondered how he would set about it, but as he did not ask me to help I came to the conclusion that it was a one man job, and followed him forward merely as a spectator. Afterwards I heard that he imagined I was annoyed with him for reducing canvas so much and was refusing to have anything to do with it. He went to the bitts and undid the heel-rope of the bowsprit and then stood clear. As soon as he let go the heelrope the bowsprit flew inboard carrying the jib with it under the lee of the staysail and out of the wind so that it was easily muzzled and lowered. A gasket was passed round the sail and made fast to a cavel on the bulwarks, and when the head of the sail had been seized to the lee rigging the sail was secure and ready for hoisting when necessary. I should think that the whole evolution took less than five minutes. I then went below to sleep until I was called to get breakfast ready. As I dozed off I chuckled to think that now I knew how to reef her and how to get the jib and bowsprit off her, and that both were as easy as winking. Any fool could do it. I had already forgotten the very frightened fool who had sat shivering in the well because he hadn't got the guts to find out things for himself.

When I came on deck for the forenoon watch it was blowing a full gale, and Bill had still further reduced sail by rolling up the mainsail and tying a reef in the staysail. He had hove her to towards the end of the middle watch, and as there was nothing to do had not called me at four o'clock. He had spent most of the time below, cocking his head out every now and then to make sure no other pilot cutter was in sight—his only anxiety. The middle had been pretty awful, but as soon as the tide turned the sea had become much quieter, and there was nothing for it but to see it out where we were. I was thoroughly ashamed of my sleepy-headedness, but Bill said that he could not have slept until dawn anyhow as he was responsible for the safety of the ship. It says something for the comfort of these cutters that I had slept peace-fully for seven hours, and had no idea what was going on outside.

We had an extra good breakfast and an extra long smoke and clear up below, and then we sat in the well and watched the ship's behaviour. The wind had taken off a little but the seas were still enormous, bearing down on us in such overwhelming masses that, again and again, I felt sure she could not rise to them in time to prevent them from breaking on our decks and driving them in. What the seas had been like when the wind was against the tide I could not imagine, and I devoutly hoped that the sea would moderate before the ebb started. One nuisance was that our topsides were leaky, and for the first time we had to use the pump to free her from the considerable amount of bilge water that had collected. This is one of the great drawbacks of oak topsides. Although this wood has great strength and durability it is a most unsuitable material for use in a position where it is alternately wet and dry. The wood swells with the damp and contracts with the dry exposure and spews the caulking very quickly. All the cutters I examined suffered from this defect, but the owners stuck to oak as the only wood that stood up to the rough work they were called upon to endure. I made a mental note at the time, 'No oak topsides for me, thank you,' and experience in later years has confirmed this opinion very strongly.

The wind had not taken off much at the turn of the tide and for four hours the deck was a perfect misery, although we were snug enough down below while the ship soaked herself to windward in a remarkable fashion. So well did the ebb carry us that late that evening we were under the lee of Lundy and, for the time at any rate, our troubles were over. Bill was glad to arrive as he had feared the steamer might get there before us, and there would be a fine old row if the pilot had to be put on board another vessel. Most emphati-cally that was one of the things that were not done. I thought we might have anchored off Lundy, and saved the work of constantly watching the ship, but this was inadvisable as the steamer might appear at any moment, and it would take too long to weigh, make sail, and go out to meet her.

The wind took off, the sea died down, and the pilot was picked up by Bill in the dinghy. It was not unusual for the pilot to put himself on board the steamer, which ran down to leeward so as to make an easy job of it. As the pilot mounted the accommodation ladder he kicked the dinghy off, and after the steamer had got out of the way we ran down and picked it up. In fine smooth weather the dinghy was hoisted on board by a Spanish burton from the masthead, but this was impossible when there was any sea as the swinging about threatened to smash the boat against the ship's side or carry away the sling. On such occasions we opened the door in the bulwarks, and both of us got hold of the nose of the dinghy and hauled her inboard by main strength.

The boat was a twelve-footer, heavily built of larch, and when we were manhandling her one day I said to Bill that this was one job he could not do by himself. He always got ratty if one suggested that there was any job on board that he could not do, and he rose to it this time by shouting that he could get the boat on board any time he liked by himself no matter what the weather was like. I laughed and told him not to brag, or rather, in the popular phrase at sea, that he was drawing too much water. He got quite angry and said he would show me one day, but it must be when the Old Man was not on board as he objected to the chance of smashing the dinghy and leaving him without transport to a waiting ship. I reminded him of his bragging one day when we were returning after putting the pilot on board a ship. Bill's answer was to jump up from the helm, open the doorway in the bulwarks and push the dinghy into the ditch after bending a stout painter to a shackle in her forefoot. The painter was marked at a spot near the dinghy, and at this mark was made fast to the boom at a place where there was a scratch in the wood. He then fixed a triangular sausage-shaped fender along the doorway outside the ship and resting against the topstrake of the cutter's side. We were running at the time with the boom pinned in and the peak halliard eased off a little, the usual trim of the mainsail when off the wind, so the peak was set up and the topping lift slacked away.

The mainsheet was then run out until the dinghy was towing alongside with its nose nearly level with the after end of the doorway opening. Bill then took the helm and steadied her for a moment, and then suddenly jibed her over by putting the helm hard up. The boom and the alteration, of course, dragged the nose of the dinghy round so that she was pointing straight for our beam, and when the boom went over with a crash it lifted the bow of the dinghy in the air and it fairly leapt into the cutter without touching anything except the fender. As soon as Bill saw that the boat was on its way he jumped from the tiller, and seizing the stern of the boat wrenched it violently round so that it came to rest alongside the bulwarks at the opposite side of the ship. He lashed it in position and came aft. 'What do you think of that?'

'I'm not surprised that you don't do it when the Old Man is about. The least slip and the boat would have been over the other side or hopelessly smashed.'

'Well, I've never smashed a boat yet, and I always get them in like that when I want to.'

For over a month this was the life we led. There was the same sea work, sometimes in fine weather, but oftener there was a gale of wind as befitted the season. At times I almost forgot that this was not my real life and, during the spells on shore, listened sympathetically to the tales of hardship and the tricks of examiners as if to me also they were the only things in the world that mattered. A kindly opinion was often given that I would have no difficulty in passing for a pilot's certificate once I had completed the requisite term of apprenticeship.

Then one day Bill and I received a shock. It seemed that our pilot had been told by the captain of a large steamer paying big pilotage fees that if he would be off the Tuskar on a certain day he would be picked up and taken to Liverpool in the steamer. When the ship left for Avonmouth, her ultimate destination, he would take charge as soon as they arrived in pilotage waters. The scheme was really by way of stealing a march on the other pilots, but these prearranged meetings were not unusual and they worked out in favour of everybody in turn. So we provisioned ship and made for the Tuskar light.

By the time we got there it was blowing a heavy gale from the south-west, and for two days we were hove-to as the gale was so fierce that the steamer could not leave Queenstown. The period of waiting was very boring but we suffered no great discomfort, as may be gauged from the fact that the pilot's pipe and tobacco pouch which he used to throw on the polished table in the saloon at bedtime were still there in the morning. Most of the time we were hove-to under reefed staysail only with the clew dragged flat amidships, and even under this scanty canvas she was still eating out to windward. After we had got rid of the pilot we made a smart passage back and picked up our moorings to await his return, which would not be for several days.

During this time we lived with the porter, and were well looked after by his wife and regaled with stories of the hardships of a railwayman's life by the husband. He never quite forgave Bill, who got bored with these stories and blurted out, 'I can't see what you have to complain about. You sleep in bed all night.' In the evening we used to go to the Institute for a game of billiards, and one time I dropped in just as I had come from the ship, dressed in a jersey and sea-boots. There was one man there who played a good game although I was usually a bit better. On this particular evening I thought he had beat me as he was in the nineties while I was still in the sixties. With some luck I managed to run out, and as I watched the red trickling into the hole that gave me the game I felt a hand on my shoulder, and an educated voice which had something familiar in its ring said, 'You play a very nice game of billiards, my man!' I turned to see the face of a man with whom I had been shipmates in the service. I had heard that he had come into a lot of money and estates, but did not know where he had gone. He recognized me with a 'Good God! It's Muir!' and I could see his eyes narrow as if thinking, 'This fellow has done something funny and has had to clear out of the service. He was always messing about in boats. What more natural than that he should turn to this for a living?' My main idea was that the seamen round us should not have their suspicions roused, so I said in an undertone, 'Don't talk to me just now. I'll see you outside in five minutes.' His face was full of misgiving, but when we met in a few minutes his laughter at my explanation bade fair to give the show away to any chance listener. We had been walking along the road while we talked, and suddenly he pushed his arm through mine, and when we came to some large iron gates leading to a drive he dragged me through them in spite of my protestations, and went up the drive. It was a long drive, but finally we came to a house with wide-spreading lawns. He opened the door, strode across the hall and flung open the door of a big Victorian drawing room. Seated in an armchair beside the fire, and busy knitting, was a beautiful white-haired old lady, while a girl was writing letters at a nearby table. The whole scene spoke of warmth and luxurious living. I was pushed in front of the old lady and introduced. 'Mother, allow me to present to you Staff-Surgeon Muir of His Majesty's Royal Navy.'

The old lady looked at my tousled gingery hair, my weatherbeaten face, my jersey, and, finally, at my not too clean seaboots, and then stared helplessly at her son, plainly asking what the joke was. The girl had broken into peals of laughter which did not help my embarrassment much. Explanations followed, and they proved the kindest and most considerate of friends, but I saw, and managed to make them see, that, in the circumstances, it was wiser to decline the invitations they showered on me. The social dividing line is drawn very rigidly in these country villages, and in those days even more harshly than now. Any crossing of the line made the offender liable to be viewed with suspicion and dislike.

From the daily paper I learned that my ship had left Malta, and I knew that my recall could not be long delayed. When it did come it came suddenly. We had put the pilot on board a homeward bounder and were to pick him up from an outward bound ship in a few days. In the meantime, we went to Ilfracombe for water and provisions and as usual went into the inner harbour and grounded on our legs. Bill and I were seated on the rail at low tide when I saw a telegraph boy wandering over the beach and reading the names of the cutters. When he came to our ship his quest seemed to be ended, and he called out to Bill, 'Have you got a staff-sergeant on board?' Bill laughed as he answered, 'No! no! sonny, there ain't no soldiers on board this ship. We're sailors we are.' But I guessed the boy's misreading of my official designation and asked him, 'Is the name Muir?' 'I think so,' said the boy. 'Then hand it up. It is for me, I expect.' It was in the usual service terms ordering me to report myself on board my ship at Portsmouth in three days' time, and requesting the usual acknowledgment. I wrote out the reply and handed it to the boy, who disappeared.

Then I turned to Bill who had been staring dumbfounded at the proceedings, and told him I must get away at once, but he refused to consider it, and told me he could do nothing without the permission of the pilot. In his opinion all I had to do was to wire back to the government people and say that I had a job and they must find someone else. I assured him that what he suggested was impossible, and as he still refused to believe me I had to make a clean breast of the whole affair in order to get him to understand how things stood. My explanation woke a bitter side to his character.

'So you've been making a fool of us all this time.'

'I haven't been making a fool of anyone.' 'Yes you have, pretending you were a sailor when all the time you were a nob.' 'I'm not a nob.'

'Yes you are. All officers are nobs.'

I was getting angry. 'Well, they're not snobs anyway.' But my shaft failed to pierce.

'I never could quite make you out. You read funny books, and got on a lot too well with the real nobs.'

Evidently my visit to the Manor House had been noted and commented upon, though I hardly think Shakespeare deserved the epithet of 'funny'.

'I did my job all right, and that is the only thing that concerns you. It was agreed that I was only temporary and free to go as soon as the other fellow was all right again.'

He saw just as far as his lights went. 'I must say you did your job all right. What I can't stand is the deceit of it.'

'You know perfectly well I have never deceived you by a single word, but if you are going on like this I'll step over the side now and you can go to the devil.'

It was impossible to remove his sense of grievance but, finally, he wired to the pilot for instructions, and the answer came back that we were to return to our moorings and pick up the regular hand who had recovered sufficiently to rejoin. We sailed as soon as the tide served. It was not a pleasant trip. There were too many references to nobs and their imagined ways of doing things, and I was feeling sore that a man I admired intensely would not allow us to part as firm friends. I was too sick of the whole business to explain matters to the porter and his wife, but Bill had evidently been giving them his version while I was packing, and there was a shadow between us when I said good-bye. The only pleasant episode came from the little girl who insisted on kissing me and said shyly, 'I always knew you were a gent from the way you spoke to mother.' The porter carried my bag this time but refused the shilling I offered him.

During one of our spells in harbour I went to see one of the famous builders of pilot cutters to discuss with him the possibility of having one built for myself. I suggested some modifications of the standard pattern, and he told me that he built all his ships from a half model. He produced this model, listened carefully to all I had to say, and then, remarking that it seemed to him I wanted a yacht more than a pilot cutter, got out a chisel and whittled away, very skilfully, until he had produced the shape I wanted. I am very doubtful whether the completed vessel would have strictly conformed to the model, as his methods of taking off were very haphazard, and the result was more influenced by the wood he had in stock than a slavish adherence to lines. He told me that he could build a cutter about fifty feet over all for £350, hull, spars, and blocks, and fitted up down below in pilot fashion. It sounds cheap and was cheap, much too cheap to allow the materials used to be of good quality.

That was the greatest objection I had to those wonderful vessels. I was inclined to believe that not a single one of them could stand a rigid survey after ten years' service, and it was only necessary to poke your head down the hatch of most of them to learn, from the unmistakable odour of rotting wood, that they were far gone in decay. After building costs had been paid the pilots expected to spend about three hundred pounds more on equipment, but this was done in the cheapest possible manner. As possible yachts I saw no attraction in them. Their most obvious faults were that, with a few notable exceptions, they were much undercanvassed, and, therefore, painfully slow in light winds, and driving them to windward made heavy going as their over-ballasting made them outrageously wet. The duty they were built for, keeping the sea in any weather, they fulfilled to a degree never equalled by any other type of small vessel.

XII

'Mynah'

U NLESS YOU HAVE TRIED you can have no idea how difficult it is to find a suitable vessel for your requirements, and especially so when your purse and your inclination insist that the ship must be small enough to be handled by one man, and that man yourself. The difficulty is great enough if you are prepared to buy, but if you only want to charter for a short period you may consider yourself fortunate if you can come across something that will float. After being led astray by numerous tom-fool advertisements I was lucky enough to find, lying on the beach at Leigh-on-Sea, a ten-ton cutter which was not only in good condition but also promised a degree of comfort down below that I was not accustomed to expect in small yachts. This comfort was due to the fact that she had been originally built for hire service on the Broads, and obviously any defects these vessels may have as seagoing propositions must be hers also. All yachts are a compromise between various desirable qualities, and the perfect ship which combines the lot of them will never be built as many of them are directly antagonistic. My choice on this particular occasion was bound to be a bad seaboat as her very shallow draught would make her useless in turning to windward except in absolutely smooth water, while the enormous coach roof which justified its existence in the spacious cabins below made her very unhandy to work. As I meant to use her for cruising in the Thames in order to increase my knowledge of that fascinating estuary, the latter drawback seemed of minor importance, while her other qualities promised a holiday of unalloyed delight. When you have experienced the greatest comfort a small yacht can give—a separate sleeping cabin—you will not go back to sleeping on the saloon settees if you can help it.

Another of her luxuries was a coal stove and, as my cruising was to be done in the month of May when the weather can be as cold as November, I looked forward to snug anchorages in shallow creeks. While the wind and rain whistled I would poke that fire and be glad I had sense enough to come in out of the wet. She carried a lot of fresh water, and there was plenty of room for stores so that I could fill her up and be independent of the shore for a week if I wanted. She was in charge of Mr. Turnnidge, and he promised to have her ready by the time I wanted, and I told him I would join her on a certain day.

One of the Barracks' steamboats which had a job to do down that way was to put me and my gear on board, and I went to sleep the night before embarkation full of the joys of the days to come. The joys were somewhat discounted the next morning when I got a message from the Commander asking whether I really meant to go that day as it was blowing a westerly gale, and the passage across from Garrison Point would be pretty lively. As far as he was concerned the launch could do the trip any other day convenient for me, and it was up to me to say whether he was to cancel the order. I knew that I had been talking in the mess about my projected trip and that the Commander who loved to rot me about my busman's holidays was expecting me to funk and say that the weather was too bad for the steamboat, really meaning, as he would be at some pains to explain, that the gale was too strong for my weak nerves. The answer I gave was that I would be ready as soon as the boat, and an hour later we were on our way down the Medway.

As long as we were in that river there was nothing to complain about, but as we went through the Jenkin Swatch the Thames was at its wildest and wickedest. Towards Leigh there was some shelter, and as it was about high water we made straight for the *Mynah* which was lying at single anchor off the town. The transfer of my gear was a bit of a job as both boats were sending heavily, and the coxswain's face was a study in mute protest at being involved in any way in such a proceeding. His manner suggested that his respect for my sanity would be considerably increased if I adopted his suggestion and went back to the Barracks in the launch, but on my refusal his interest in the matter ended, and I am sure his tongue was in his cheek when he saluted and wished me a pleasant holiday. I have come across many naval officers of all ranks who looked on yachting, even in the smallest vessels, as the ideal holiday, but I never met a lower-deck rating who did not regard it as a stupid waste of time. 'You don't gets nowhere, and there's nothing to do when you gets there anyhow,' was the opinion of a retired petty officer whom I employed as a temporary hand.

The wife of another was even more emphatic when I offered to take him away with me for a few days. He said he would be glad to come if I could square his missus. I saw the lady and had no difficulty with her at all. I had barely broached the subject of breaking up her happy home when she assented vigorously. 'Yes. You take him and keep him as long as you like. It'll teach him to appreciate his good home when he comes back.' Evidently the popular notion among wives is that yachting involves the most extraordinary hardships. The other idea is that yachting is a life of bloated luxury only to be indulged in by the fabulously wealthy. Most yachtsmen who handle their own ships will agree that neither extreme falls to their lot except on rare occasions.

But I am standing on the deck of the *Mynah*, which is behaving in a manner that has always made me bless the fact that I have a seaproof stomach. On one occasion we were running hard in front of a north-east gale, coming back from Holland, and towards dinner-time my thoughts turned with affection to an excellent stew which had been prepared the day before and only wanted warming up. I gave the helm to Vincent and went to the fo'c'sle, which was battened down, lit the Rippingille, and had a jolly good dinner. When it was over I sent Vincent below to feed, but he came back in less than five minutes and he did not look any too happy. On inquiring whether the stew was to his liking, he admitted he had hardly tasted it, so I told him to go back and finish his dinner. He said he was not going back for anybody or any tinted dinner. It had not struck me that even his seasoned stomach had succumbed, so I asked him what was the matter. He made a brief visit to the side of the ship, the first for twenty years, and then blurted out: 'How you could stand the smell in that fo'c'sle I don't know. I don't call it hardly human down there.' All because a little paraffin had been jolted out of the stove reservoirs!

As the tide ebbed the sea got less, and I was able to get on with some of the work of stowing the gear and getting ready for sailing. It was impossible to leave the anchorage in this weather until I had learned something about the boat and her behaviour. When the tide had fallen sufficiently I was introduced to a new experience as the keel began to thump on the hard sand. She came down with such a whack that I feared lest she would be seriously damaged, so much so that as soon as she had dried out sufficiently to let me get ashore I dashed off to Mr. Turnnidge to get him to come and have a look at her. But I was laughed at. She would take no harm. All the Leigh bawleys grounded in the same way and never took any harm, and *Mynah* had been specially strengthened to stand the same sort of treatment. She had been thumped like that for years and had never been a penny the worse. I took his word for it, but at two next morning when she was taking the ground again I began to think that dawn would find me perched like a gull at the masthead of a sunken ship. Twice I went to the pump, certain that her bottom must be stove in, but did not find anything to worry about. It seemed to me to be a good omen for the times when I might get aground by accident.

Next morning I was tired of being knocked about when the tide was up, thumped when the ship was taking the ground, and lying over at an uncomfortable angle in the intervals. Although the wind was as strong as ever I hauled down a couple of reefs, and having dug up my anchor, which was deeply imbedded in the sand, got away as soon as the tide had risen enough to float me. I had better have waited until the strength of the flood was done but I wanted to get that anchor well stowed and secured before I left. There was a vicious sea with the wind against tide on the way to Queenborough, which I considered was the best place to await an improvement in the weather. I went round the Nore lightship, and, as I hauled my wind to make for the entrance to the Medway, she blew to leeward like an old saucer, until I thought she was going to be carried inside the line of the Cant buoys where the riot of breaking seas would have rendered her unmanageable. I was more than thankful when I had nursed her round Garrison Point, run up the West Swale and let go amongst a crowd of storm-bound barges.

That same evening I gave a passage off in my dinghy to a couple of bargees whom I found waiting for their boat on the hard. On the way one of them said that I must have had a pretty rotten passage down the Medway, as I looked knocked about when I came in. The answer, of course, was that I had not come down the Medway, but from Leigh. They treated this as a good joke, and when I insisted that it was true, said it was no use my trying to pull their legs. Not a single barge had left the Swale for the last two days, and when that happened there was no chance of a boat like mine coming through such weather as they knew was blowing outside. I let them have it at that. The danger in barges is not that they cannot stand the weather, but they are so deeply laden that the constant water on their decks is apt to get under the tarpaulin covers of their hatches and damage their cargo. When a barge is sunk by bad weather it is nearly always for this reason, and she is said to have foundered. This is not a term in common use except in storybooks, and I heard an amusing instance of its application once.

At the mouth of Cromarty Firth a lugsail ferry-boat manned by two fishermen used to ply between the town of Cromarty and the Nigg shore. For well-defined reasons this was known throughout the Fleet as the 'drunken' ferry, and one time, along with a lieutenant, I was crossing from the Nigg side when the ferry was living up to its reputation. The lug was hoisted, and in the fresh breeze the boat was very much over-canvassed, a fact that had seemed to escape the notice of the semi-somnolent steersman. In spite of his condition he was handling his boat remarkably well, and as we had only a short distance to go I was not worrying much, but half-way across the lieutenant thought it was time to interfere. He leant across to Palinurus and shouted above the wind, 'Don't you think you are carrying too much sail? She'll capsize.' The helmsman half roused himself from his alcoholic satisfaction with the world at large, stared for a moment at the straining sail above him, pondered deeply, and then shook his head slowly and decisively. 'Na! Na! She'll no capsize.' Then he sleepily watched the maelstrom around us and felt that he had committed himself too much. He became oracular. 'Mebbee, I'm no' saying she will, but mebbee she'll foonder.' With this he resigned himself to moody contemplation of the uncertainties of a wicked world. The lieutenant caught my eye and both of us burst out laughing. Before the paroxysm was over the insulted crew were handing us out of the boat.

By the following morning the wind had died away and, in company with a string of barges which were also bound east, I left the Swale at mid-day bound for the Crouch. In spite of having the tide with me progress was painfully slow. Towards low tide I was trying to cross the Whitaker spit near to the buoy. The wind had completely gone, and I feared that the last of the ebb from the Crouch would carry me into the Swin and the young flood would take me back to Sheerness again. I went forward to let go the anchor, ranged about five fathoms of cable on the deck, and threw the sixty-pound hook over the side. For anchor work there was an old-fashioned barrel windlass and, as the anchor was not holding, I had to tighten the cable over the drum with my left hand. She must have snubbed much more quickly than I expected, for, before I realized what was happening, my left hand was caught between the cable and the drum, and blood was spouting from my finger tips. There was nothing to be done, as it was impossible to free my hand until the ship went ahead on her cable, and in those few seconds, thanks to a vivid imagination, I saw myself a cripple for life and my career as a surgeon finished. The pain, agonizing at first, went off very quickly, and by the time the cable slacked up and I got my hand free I did not feel any pain at all. This is the merciful stage of shock, experienced in all severe injuries, and I knew that for a short time I could handle and make any examination I pleased without undue pain. So I sat down on the bitts and put my hand through a piece-meal scrutiny. The result was fairly satisfactory, as no bones had been broken and the sinews were intact, but the lacerations were very severe, and the cable had impressed a very perfect pattern on the soft parts.

I have always made a point of carrying a good store of surgical dressings with me on these expeditions and, although they have often been useful, this was the first time they had been of serious use for my own injuries. As I mopped and lashed my hand up I thought of my favourite argument against single-handed sailing. The major catastrophes did not matter much as the agony is soon over, but what is really a very slight injury from the land stand-point can make it possible for an otherwise healthy person to be quite helpless on board a boat. It was on these grounds that I always warned my friends not to indulge in that form of cruising. Of course, like all doctors, I never took my own advice, and here I was an excellent example of the risks attached to the sport. There was some difficulty in stopping the bleeding, but when the hand was dressed I went on deck, took in the jib and staysail and tidied up the fore-deck, which looked as if someone had been killing sheep on it.

I was none too pleased with the general situation. The ship was anchored in the open sea and several miles from shelter. If the weather signs and the barometer were to be trusted the fine spell during the day was only tempo-rary, and a change was imminent. Darkness was shortly due, and I was sure I could not work my way up the Crouch in my crippled condition when it would be necessary to attend to the headsheets and the lead at the same time. The mainsail had been left up, but if the lightest breeze arose it would have to come down somehow. If I stayed where I was some rascal would pick me up and make me a salvage case in spite of my protestations. In fact I was in a nice mess. If it had been later in the season there would have been plenty of yachts about who would have gladly lent me a hand, but the only vessel in sight was a bawley dredging for shrimps with the tide, about half a mile away.

The bawley was driven fairly close to me, and it struck me that I might be able to induce him to lend me a hand if I pretended to be the tomfool yachts-man that most of these people quite justly imagine we are. I was helped by his remark as he came near. 'I see that you've got the old *Mynah* there.' 'Do you know her?' 'Oh yes! I know her well. She lays up at Turnnidges at Leigh.' This was encouraging, so I went on. 'Do you know a river about here called the Roach?' 'Yes I know it well, but most of the yachts go up the Crouch to Burnham.' 'But the Roach is a lot nearer, isn't it? I think I'd prefer to go there. How much would you want to pilot me up?' 'Ten shillings wouldn't hurt you, would it?' It was twice as much as he had any right to expect, but I was not in a position to argue, and, if I were the fool I wanted him to think, he was entitled to stand out for the higher sum. 'All right, I'll pay you that much with pleasure.' As the tide swept him out of hearing, he shouted out, 'Me and my mate was going to bring up under Holywell for the night anyway. We'll come for you as soon as the tide is done.'

Well that was settled and one of my chief anxieties was removed, but it was dark and beginning to blow before he came alongside and jumped on board. He seemed to take it for granted that I did not offer to help him in setting the canvas or getting the anchor up, and I told him that I would steer if he would keep the lead going, as he knew the ground better than I did. He agreed to this, and, with his mate in the bawley following closely in our tracks, we worked up to Foulness, keeping the lead going all the time. After that the rest was easy, though he looked like arguing when he found that I had very definite ideas about where I meant to anchor in the Roach when we turned into that river. I then asked him to stow the canvas for me, and was able to give him sufficient help to avoid arousing any suspicion. It was when we went into the saloon to get the money for payment that I was unmasked. In lighting the cabin lamp he saw my bandaged hand and that I had left some blood on the chimney.

'What's the matter with your hand?'

'Nothing much. I got it in the windlass when I was letting go off the Whitaker.'

'I thought there was something funny about you when we were coming up and that you knew the river as well as I did. If I had known that your hand was like that I wouldn't have brought you up for five pounds.'

'Yes, I know you wouldn't, and it's salvage sharks like you that give decent fishermen a bad name at sea. Not content with good payment for an easy job you try to get a great deal more than your services are worth by calling them salvage. I was prepared to stay where I was until my hand was all right, or until my provisions ran out rather than pay a penny of salvage to anyone.'

He looked uneasy at my outburst, and did not feel attracted by my picture of salvage as seen by the salvaged.

'I thought you was a mug when you said you would give me ten bob, when you must have known that if you had said five shillings I would have taken it.' He scratched his head ruefully. 'I'm the mug all right.'

'Look here!' I said. 'I must stay here until my hand is fit for work again. If you lay out my kedge for me and give me a harbour stow I'll give you another ten bob and five shillings for your mate.'

He brightened up at that, and proceeded to do what he was told. Right well he did it too, and suggested a lot of things to make the work easier for me. When it was finished he called to his mate in the bawley which had anchored near us, and as they rowed away I heard him telling his mate with delight. 'Called me a salvage shark he did! And me thinking he was a mug!'

That night as I twisted with pain in my bunk and heard the wind whistling through the rigging I was thankful I was anchored close up to a weather shore and not rolling and plunging off the Whitaker buoy. Just before dawn the clank of a windlass told me that the bawley was getting under way, and I slipped out and shouted goodbye, which received a cheery response and an inquiry whether they could do anything for me before they left. To my suggestion that they might tell Mr. Turnnidge when they got back to Leigh that they had wanted to make a salvage case of the *Mynah* they sent back a roar of laughter.

The ensuing three weeks were the most peaceful and in some ways the happiest I have ever spent. At first the hand was painful, but when that stage had passed all I had to do was to find out the easiest ways of looking after myself with only one efficient hand. There were only a few operations which I was never able to master. For instance I never learned how to tie my shoelaces or my cravat, and I never became an expert at striking a match and lighting a cigarette. For the first week an old fisherman whom I hailed when passing brought me such local supplies as I needed, but after that I rigged the sailing dinghy and managed to fend for myself. The dressings I had with me ran short and the old man told me of a district nurse at Foulness. She supplied my wants and expended much unnecessary pity on my forlorn and damaged condition. The time passed very quickly. For a few hours on Sunday afternoons half a dozen small yachts from Burnham anchored near me, but for the rest of the week I had the river to myself. Lying in my bunk at bedtime I fell asleep to the mournful call of the curlews, and each morning was waked by the same old gull which sat on the cabin skylight and wailed like a hungry baby, the note gradually dying away to one of querulous satisfaction. The weather was perfect May, and though I regretted the loss of sailing there was no great sorrow for the deprivation. I only once sailed the dinghy to Burnham, but my crippled state made me the object of so much unsolicited and hopeful attention that I did not repeat the visit. I have never appreciated that depth of avarice in which the misfortunes of others are looked upon as an opportunity for exaggerating the value of services rendered.

One joyful morning I woke to the knowledge that the abrasions were nearly healed, and that, with the exception of a split thumb which was never to recover completely, there was nothing that a stout glove could not protect sufficiently if I wanted to get away. With the help of the fisherman I weighed the anchor and kedge and sailed for the Blackwater, as I was anxious to explore the upper reaches of that river.

There was only time for a short visit, and when that was over I must return to Chatham from where the yacht was to be sent back to Leigh. The voyage through the Rays'n and up the river was peaceful and tedious, and it was not until late in the evening that I let go abreast of a little wooden pier on Osea Island. I knew nothing about the place and was surprised to see what looked like a large hotel on this remote and rather desolate spot. There seemed to be a large number of male visitors and several of them got into small boats which were lying at the pier and pulled round the ship. They were all very well dressed and were unusually friendly, hanging on to the ship's side and chatting about the weather and other subjects of common interest. As it was late and I had a meal to cook I did not offer the usual yachtsman's hospitality and ask them on board for a drink. After a little they faded away and I saw no more of them. The next morning a barge yacht was lying near to me, and by and by two men came across from her for a yarn and to borrow a loaf as they had been stranded in Goldhanger creek for some days and unable to get ashore. In the course of our talk I asked how an hotel in the situation of the one on shore could pay, as I did not think there were any attractions for visitors, and yet the place seemed fairly full. I told my experience of the previous evening. One of the men laughed and told me the following story.

Some years ago he was exploring the Thames in the barge yacht along with two friends, and after a rotten day of punching against head winds they anchored in their present position. Their wearied and drenched spirits were delighted to see an hotel nestling amongst the trees. They reasoned that where there is an hotel there is food, and good food too, and their dear hearts rejoiced. As it was a bit late it was decided that one of them had better go ashore and tell the hotel people to keep something hot for them, and the others were to follow as soon as the ship was cleared up. The prospect of a good dinner cheered the others up—as all they had hoped for was to knock the head off a tin—while the third man dashed ashore in the dinghy, fearful lest dinner was over for the day. He rang the bell, but got no answer, so he pushed open the door and entered the hall, in semi-darkness and only lit by the afterglow. He made his way to a man who was coming down the stairs and asked whether dinner was over. The man said it was, and added, 'And a damned good dinner too.'

'Well, do you think my two friends could have some of that dinner? We have just come in in a yacht and we are sorry we are a bit late.'

'No! You can't have any dinner here.'

The yachtsman thought he had got hold of the manager, and tried to appeal to his feelings, so went on:

'I know it's asking rather a lot if you have cleared up, but we have had a bad time and we are all very hungry. We won't look for very much, but you might let us have something, and we are prepared to pay well for what we get.'

The only result of this heartfelt appeal was another refusal in the same terms. Then the yachtsman began to get annoyed as he thought of the reception he would get on board if he failed to announce that a meal was waiting for the others. Being a lawyer he knew that by its licence an hotel is compelled to provide reasonable refreshment, and he became firm.

'I demand that according to the terms of your licence you provide us with refreshment. This is an hotel, isn't it?'

The man protruded his face towards the inquirer, and all the bitterness of hope long deferred was in his voice, as he shouted, 'I wish to God it was!'

The place was an inebriates' home!

XIII

The Spitway Bell Buoy

THE WELL-KNOWN HOSPITALITY of the local Yacht Club had been too much to my liking to induce me to punch to windward in heavy seas, but now that the weather had moderated it was necessary to get away before the powers who controlled my leave in Chatham fetched me back as a deserter. So one summer's evening, just before the war, the *Chula* was lying in the yacht harbour at Lowestoft, 'in all respects ready for sea', whither we proposed to proceed at dawn the following morning. I was walking up and down the deck while my hand was setting the jib in stops, when I noticed a forlorn-looking group consisting of a youth and two girls standing on the pier, where my stern warps were fastened to a bollard, gazing listlessly at my ship. She was a ship well worth looking at; at least in pride of recent ownership I thought so, and if these people knew anything about yachts I was sure they were envying me in their hearts. To me, therefore, it was not in the least surprising that the youth remarked as I reached the counter a few feet below the level of the spot where they were standing: 'You're a very lucky man to have a ship like that.' I made the usual reply of all yachtsmen whose hearts have been warmed by a sympathetic gesture: 'Glad you think so. Come on board and have a look at her if you can spare the time.' He spoke to the two girls, one about sixteen and the other about twenty as I guessed, and apparently had some difficulty in getting them to agree to accept the invitation. After a little discussion in an undertone they signified their willingness, and I sent the dinghy in to the landing-place to fetch them. They were all extraordinarily awkward at getting into the boat, and nearly capsized Coxton into the ditch when I helped them up the gangway ladder.

From the outset the visit threatened to be a complete failure. It was plain that none of them knew anything about yachts, and the listless uninterested attitude of the two elders made the work of entertaining very heavy going. Down below things were made a little easier by the younger girl, who was delighted with the living accommodation, and looked on the whole arrangement as a glorified doll's house. She asked all sorts of shrewd questions as to the internal economy, itched to open drawers and cupboards, examined bunks and folding washstands, asked me if I were ever seasick, and behaved liked a child presented with a new and fascinating toy. The others had subsided on the saloon settees whilst I was brought back again and again to explain some gadget. Finally she sank, breathless with excitement, on a seat, and exclaimed, 'It is just like Heaven!'

It had never struck me that an eighteen-ton yawl, especially in a seaway, had the remotest resemblance to Heaven, but the enthusiasm for the little ship was so spontaneous and flattering that I felt strongly inclined to let them see how ideal she could be, and, making some excuse, I slipped into the forecastle where Coxton was already at work, and told him I wanted to ask these people to stay to supper. 'Could he manage it?'

I ought to have mentioned that Coxton was a good cook, and fancied himself a much better one. The last time he jibed the ship all standing, smashed the mainboom, tore the mainsail, and ran me up a bill for £25 for repairs, I called him several different things as well as the progeny of a sea-cook, and advised him to seek office somewhere as a scullion for which I could heartily recommend him. He took my advice and is now the chef on a large liner.

His reply was encouraging. 'Manage it? Of course I can. Unless they have been starving for a fortnight.'

I went back to the saloon and made my proposal. It was received in dead silence, and for a moment I felt horribly uncomfortable and afraid lest, unintentionally, I had transgressed the formal code of politeness of my very short-lived acquaintances. The elder girl to whom I had naturally addressed my invitation looked helplessly at the others, who made no effort at helping her to come to a decision, and finally stammered: 'Yes! I should think—You don't know us—We should be so pleased—Not put you to any trouble—You can't have made any preparations for so many.'

Of course I said it was all right. No trouble. Always cooked a lot of stuff before going to sea in case the weather prevented it later. Jolly glad if they would stay.

They stayed. But where the relations between myself and the two elders had been uneasy before, they were appallingly difficult now, and even the younger girl had become silent and reserved, and would barely answer any attempt at conversation. I did not know what to make of them, but I sent the girls into the after-cabin to wash and tidy up, and tried to tempt the youth with a glass of sherry which he refused. His expression puzzled me. After a little I found myself comparing him to a trapped rabbit, and thinking: 'Dash it all, if I can't give him as good a meal as he expects to get at home he needn't look as if he thought I was going to poison him.' Coxton came into the saloon to light the lamp and lay the table for supper, and, as he did so, the girls came in from the after-cabin. They had taken off their hats and coats, and I could see and judge them better. They were by the grace of God as well as by the consent of man what, for want of a better term, are usually called ladies. They immediately went to Coxton's assistance, much to that misguided youth's amusement, as he proceeded to indicate the resting-places of the various articles required in the most nautical terms he could muster.

We sat down to supper, and I will say, for the credit of the present super-marine chef, that it was a good one—in fact much better than the idle rascal would have bothered to provide for his employer. In some strange fashion he had managed to provide quantity as well, which made me rather uneasy as to what I was to feed on during the next two days of our passage up the Thames.

Supper was a much pleasanter meal than at one time had seemed likely. We were all young and had good appetites, and some of the gloom which had attended the earlier part of the evening was dispelled. I spent most of the time at my favourite game of guessing the social position of those whom chance had thrown in my way, but these three defeated me every time I thought I had come to a definite conclusion. They were not the usual type of seaside visitor, and their conversation and accent were not local in any way. They reminded me of someone, but of whom I could not fathom. The youth was completely

In all respects ready for sea

beyond me. I had never in my limited experience met anyone quite like him before. As they were all good friends, calling one another by their first names, a rare custom in those days, the original impression they had given me of settled misery became more mysterious than ever.

Girls rarely smoked in those days, and they refused the cigarettes I offered after supper had been cleared away. The youth and I lit up, and conversation had again become difficult. I racked my brains to think of something to say, and finally, I turned to the child, who was sitting on the settee beside me, and, remembering her interest in the domestic details of the life on board, remarked: 'I hope you enjoyed your supper. You see, with only the two of us on board, and lots of other things to do as well, we don't go in for anything very elaborate in the way of meals.'

To my intense astonishment she coloured up to the roots of her hair, her lips moved tremulously, as if she were making an effort at reply, her eyes filled with tears, and then she suddenly dropped her head in her hands and sobbed as if her heart would break. I was aghast. What had I said in my feeble attempt at making conversation to bring about such a scene? I looked helplessly across the table at the other two, but they were gazing at the sobbing girl with a curiously immobile, rigid stare that was almost inhuman in its complete detachment. They neither stirred nor spoke until I blurted out: 'I am very sorry. I must have said something that has been misunderstood. Please explain that to her.' There was no reply, and I reached across the narrow table and shook the youth by the shoulder. This time I demanded, 'I insist on an explanation. What is the matter with her?' The youth this time looked at me, still in that horrible detached manner, and spoke as if he were repeating a lesson learned by rote. 'What is the matter with her is that this is the first decent meal any of us has had for a week, and the only one of any kind we have had to-day.'

He dropped his eyes for a moment and then went on: 'And now having told you this we must thank you for your generous hospitality and go.' He and his companion stood up, and I followed their example, my brain seething in a whirl of protest. The thing was fantastic. Here in my comfortable saloon were three nice-looking, well-educated, reasonably well-dressed youngsters telling me that they were starving, and, as I recollected their lassitude and apathy, I was being compelled to believe them. The child had not moved, but, with her head buried in her arms on the table, was still sobbing, but by this time in a forlorn, pathetic fashion that was more than I could stand. 'You have either said too much or too little.' They were swaying with weakness and weariness as they stood. Fool that I was, it is my job to know these things at sight, and it had been in front of me all evening and I had never guessed. 'Sit down and let me think.'

Thanks to my Scottish ancestry I have a limited strain of shrewdness in my character and, in spite of the evidence to the contrary, the thought would obtrude that I was being made the victim of a plant, and that the next move would be a request for a loan. I have been had that way many times, and if that were the game I thought I had wit enough to counter it. If it were not a plant, something had got to be done about it, though what that something was I had not the foggiest notion. Anyhow explanations were due.

'Now tell me what all this is about.'

He rose from his seat and gave me a bow and a flourish of his hand, the effect of which was mitigated by the proportions of the saloon.

'Sir, we are actors, and have fallen upon evil times.' That was the beginning of it, and I wish I could tell it in his own words, and with the dramatic intensity that his artistic soul felt to be its due. It was a common enough story in those days of an entertainment company which had been a failure, and they had wakened up one morning to the knowledge that the manager had levanted with all the cash after having failed to pay their wages for a fortnight, and they were left absolutely penniless. The youth had taken the hero's part (he was still the hero) in the plays they produced, the girls were singers and dancers as well as actresses. That same morning their landlady had seized the girls' luggage and had turned them into the street, and he was expecting the same fate at any moment.

My inquiries elicited that the only bond between the girls and himself was the tie of their common misfortunes. The girls were sisters and the orphan daughters of an actor, and had no friends to whom they could appeal. He imparted that the ducal house of which he was a scion had cast him out when he elected, in spite of opposition, to fulfil his destiny on the stage. They had tried everything, and had even tramped to Yarmouth, and had failed to find a job. All the summer entertainment parties were made up and there was not the faintest chance of a local engagement. Now they had no money, and no clothing, to try their luck in any of the other coast towns. At the end of the recital the old gloom returned as if it had suddenly been borne in upon him that it was his own story he was telling and not the mythical misfortunes of a stage hero. Finally, he apostrophized the beams some three feet over his head. 'Ah! If only we could get to Southend. There, in Southend, we would find salvation.'

Little devil doubt raised his head once more. I was due to sail next morning for Chatham, and, as my passage would bring me fairly close to Southend, I began to suspect a plant again. We were quite well known on the jetty and it was possible that he had heard a report that we were bound that way and thought he could wangle a passage.

'Do you know anything about yachts?'

'Nothing at all. This is the first time I have ever been on board one.'

'Then why did you make that remark on my ship when you were on the pier?'

'I apologize for that. I could not help expressing my bitterness that one man should have so much to make life worth while when I had so little. I was grateful to you immediately after for not taking it amiss, and your invitation surprised me and made the girls afraid. They have suffered much at the hands of some of the men here, but I said they were quite safe as long as I was with them.'

I thought I would try him a little.

'I can lend you the money to take you to Southend if you like.'

He looked at the girl beside him, and she shook her head.

'We are very grateful, but that sum alone would be no use. There are the lodgings to pay as well, and the whole sum is so great that we could not guarantee its return as our earnings are problematical.'

This seemed like a dead end, but by this time all my doubts were gone, and I had another string to my bow.

'I am sailing for Chatham at dawn tomorrow. It is very little out of my way to take you with me and drop you at Southend. How much would it cost to settle up with your landladies and get your luggage free?'

He named the sum, a pitifully small one, and I counted out the money at once and handed it over to him. The girls were staring open-mouthed at us.

'Now go ashore and settle up, and come back as soon as you can. I want to turn in early, as we have very little time for sleep.'

It was only while my hand was putting them ashore that I remembered they had never actually said they were coming with me. But I had lost all my doubts as to their being genuine. When Coxton came back I told him that we were going to have guests for the trip, and gave orders for my gear to be removed from the sleeping cabin and the place tidied up for the reception of the ladies. When I went in to see that everything was all right I found that he had dug out the stormpots and fitted them on the bunk leeboards. When I asked him what he meant by it he replied that they would be wanted in the Stanford Channel. I left them, and later came in for a lot of chaff from the girls, who thought they were spittoons and a reflection on their manners. I rather regretted giving up my comfortable sleeping cabin for the saloon settees, which the youth and I were to occupy, but I came to the conclusion that it was no great hardship as it would only be for a couple of nights, and I rarely used the cabin when doing the night sailing that seemed likely.

By nine o'clock they were calling out for the boat, and when they came alongside it was almost impossible to believe that they were the same people. There was much laughing and joking as they were shown their quarters, and the girls refused all help and advice as they proceeded to make hay of the sleeping cabin and remove the stormpots when they discovered their normal use. They sat in the saloon and talked for half an hour, but their yawns rapidly outran the apologizing limit, and personally I was glad when they said good night and disappeared, because I too was tired, and was anxious to get some sleep before the alarm went off at three.

But I had reckoned without my host, or in this case, without my guest. I had been puzzled by his enthusiastic reference to Southend and salvation. I knew Southend, and had a nodding acquaintance with the subjective condition called salvation, but had never heard these two things correlated before, and was anxious to know how he did it. I made one mistake in giving him a whisky and soda, which, at his own urgent request, was a very small one. He assured me that he was not accustomed to the consumption of what he called spirituous liquors, and soon I had ample evidence of the truth of his statement, as the tiny tot I gave him induced the expansive stage of intoxication in less than five minutes. Before that happened he had informed me, plausibly enough, that he had a friend working the Southend area, and that he was sure this friend could find a job for the lot of them. That, at any rate, was good hearing.

It may have been the whisky, it may have been the relief from present anxiety, it may have been the rosiness of his future prospects, or it may only have been the natural man emerging from the cloud that had almost overwhelmed him, but, as he talked, I saw that an entirely new rôle was being adopted, and his face and figure seemed to conform to the altered character. There was a sweep of his hand through his hair, a tug at his necktie, a shrugging of his shoulders, a *hey presto* pass of his hand over his face, and, sitting in front of me, I had a debonair actor as little like the rather ordinary youth who had said good night to the girls a few minutes before, as could well be imagined. It reminded me ludicrously of one of those impersonators who give their entire show without leaving the stage. He was now well up centre, and as his beautifully rounded periods gained in volume and fluency I had, perforce, to listen. There was no escape without actual rudeness, and he assumed that from a man of my standing any such action was beyond the wildest flights of fancy.

'An actor's life is a wonderful one, and I shall be glad to resume my former position of leading man. Where else, except amongst actors, can you find a man whose training and education enable him to mix equally and easily with the highest or the lowest? One night we walk the street in rags with neither a roof to shelter us nor a mite with which to buy a crust in order to assuage the pangs of hunger; the next we dine with wealthy men on board sumptuous yachts (here he bowed gravely to me, making me feel such a blithering idiot that I missed my cue if there was one) and waited upon by paid menials. Is it a bazaar that is to be opened or a funeral oration that is to be made? Then who can coax the money from the reluctant purse of the unwilling rich or sound the note that will soothe the distracted sorrower so well as the actor whose professional life has taught him to depict the joys and sorrows of all kinds and conditions of men? Did I say we act? We do not act, we feel, or our interpretation of our parts is feeble and unconvincing. When we are kings our thoughts are as royal as our robes or actions; if we are beggars we are abased and the dust of defilement is our portion. Have you never noticed this, you whose feet have always trod the primrose paths of prosperity?'

It was the first chance I had of cutting in, and I am ashamed to say I took it, although I have an idea I was not really meant to.

'No, I can't say I have noticed. Have another drink.'

The divine fire had passed. We turned in and slept.

The Stanford Channel was on its best behaviour after all when we negotiated it early next morning. There was a light north-west wind, ideal in direction, but disappointing in strength, and promising anything but a quick passage. Indeed the ship was so quiet that it was only the call of breakfast at eight o'clock that brought my sleepy-headed guests on deck. The view of the Suffolk coast spread out before them towards Dunwich was beautiful, but it could not compete with the aroma of bacon and eggs and coffee, and we sat down with appetites sharpened by the fresh sea air.

I had expected to see very little of them on the passage, and had not made any preparations to help beguile the time away. They all steered for a bit, but soon got bored with that tedious occupation in a light wind. Later they just lay about the deck and got horribly in the way as all newcomers on board a small yacht do. At one time they explored my nautical library, but sailing directions provided poor excitement, and almanacs failed to arouse any interest. I had none of the novels which seemed to be their favourite literature.

The youth found my Shakespeare and, with intervals for refreshment, buried himself in that for the rest of the day. They asserted that they were quite happy, but I am sure that in their hearts they were all longing for the so-called blessings of the land.

By the end of the tide we had struggled past Orford Ness, and then our progress was very slow. The wind had a tendency to veer to the east and fall lighter. That meant fog for a certainty as night fell, and the prospect of being caught in the crowded Barrow Deep in a fog and very light breeze was so unattractive that I made up my mind to take the channel known as the Wallet, and pass into the East Swin by means of the Wallet Spitway. By taking this route I was not likely to meet with anything more formidable than one of the local fishing boats, and the damage sustained would be more moral than material. One of my most persistent nightmares is the sudden appearance of a forty-foot steel prow aiming straight at my midships section.

The day passed slowly, the tide ebbed and flowed, meals appeared and were consumed at their appointed times, my guests idled and yawned, and finally, about ten, they decided to turn in. I knew that we were somewhere round about the Naze, but although I had kept a careful reckoning I had not been able to check my position by shore bearings since we had passed one of the Cutler buoys early in the afternoon. Then the fog had shut down and we had carried with us a little circular world about a quarter of a mile in diameter, in which we were the only object visible as we moved over the surface of the placid water. Now with darkness the sky was clear overhead, while the fog was of that quality in which one is certain to see wraithly figures of one's imagination appearing every time you try to pierce the filmy veil. On the port hand could be heard the wailing protests of ships against the conditions under which they were compelled to navigate, while the regularly spaced groans from the light vessels gave warning of the dangers of the narrow channels.

At first my guests were alarmed by the sudden blares so close at hand, but when I had explained that a rampart of sand effectually protected us they lost all interest, and my experiments with the lead roused only a languid attention. Of its significance they had not the faintest notion although they were surprised to learn that though we were apparently far out at sea there was only a depth of less than forty feet. I was glad when they settled down, and hoped they would not give me any trouble when we left the empty channel and joined the hooting throng in the Swin. I still remember with terror being nearly run down by a liner when piloting a crippled motor-yacht. At the critical moment, when there was urgent need for the possession of all my faculties if disaster were to be avoided, a shrieking girl got me round the neck with both arms and implored me to save her. I did save her, but she liked my method of rescue so little that she never spoke to me again.

The tide was due to flood about two a.m., and towards that time I believed that I must be nearing the Spitway passage. This channel runs very nearly north and south across the Gunfleet sand and is the only route for small vessels making for the East Swin. It is marked on the north by a spherical buoy, and on the south by a buoy with a bell, the tolling of the bell being caused by the movement of the buoy as it rolls in the swell of the sea. Neither buoy was lighted at this time and the sea was so calm that it was possible the motion was insufficient to sound the bell. The spitway is narrow, and if I altered course too soon I would inevitably drive the ship on the sand, as it rises so steeply on that side that the lead gives little or no warning. If I missed the channel the tide would sweep me up the Blackwater, and, with so light an easterly breeze, it would be impossible to beat back. I had cruised in the Thames long enough to have a horror of stranding as, though the rising tide may get you off without any damage, the ship will pound to bits on the rock-like hardness of the sand if the sea gets up while you are still aground. I had plenty to think about as I sat on my deck-stool and steered, while Coxton lay on his face on the foredeck and kept a look-out.

There was a scuffling noise in the companion and the head and shoulders of the younger girl appeared in the misty moonlight. She started when she saw me close to her, and exclaimed, 'It's you! I thought you had all gone to bed.' I laughed. 'How did you think the ship was going to be looked after if everybody is asleep?'

'I thought you always anchored at night. Haven't you been in bed at all? Are you going to stay up all night?'

'Looks like it,' I answered, though her words set me thinking. Long ago I had been present at a Court of Enquiry on an officer who was accused of 'stranding and hazarding' one of Her Majesty's ships in a fog. He was only asked two questions by the President of the Court, but they damned him for life.

'When the fog came on so thickly that navigation was attended with danger, were you in anchorage waters?'

'Yes.'

'Why did you not anchor?'

No reply that would have satisfied a seaman was possible, and the officer knew this and made no effort at any excuse. My case was similar. I could easily anchor where I was, but if I did it meant the loss of twelve hours' tide and the probable result of that loss of time would make me a leave-breaker. As no excuse except illness is accepted for this offence the penalty might affect the whole of my future career. There was nothing for it but to go on. Whatever happened to the ship I need not face a Naval Court of Enquiry, although my insurance people might have something unpleasant to say about it.

I turned to the girl: 'What are you doing on deck? You ought to be in bed yourself.'

'I've slept so much all day that I couldn't sleep in bed, and I could get a glimpse of the moon through the skylight. I thought I would like to come up and enjoy it. Do you want me to go back?'

'No,' I said, 'stay up if you want to. But get some warm things on. You'll find it a bit chilly up here.'

She disappeared, and in a few minutes came up and sat down beside me. Overhead the big mainsail was gently swaying with a patter of reef points, while the masthead traced an arc amongst the stars. The woolly mist surrounded us and a vagrant moonbeam marked the passing of the swell under the ship which nodded lazily to the disturbance. She shivered as she looked around.

'Isn't it lonely out here?'

'Lonely!' I said. 'This isn't lonely. There's the sky above you and the sea all around. There's Coxton up forrard and me sitting here. There's the ship beneath your feet which, if only you have the ears to listen, will tell you more fairy tales than Hans Andersen ever dreamt of, and some that not even he could write.' A siren suddenly blared forth its warning note followed immediately by a succession of three blasts in a different key. 'Do you know what that is? It means that two ships in the main channel have seen one another and are hastily altering course so as to avoid collision. Listen! That is the Barrow Deep lightship, and that is the Swin Middle. And all those other sounds you hear are the little ships. Think of all that these ships mean. Think of all the places they are going to and the cargoes they are carrying. And, above everything, think of the men on the alert who are driving them through this fog, the adventures they may meet, the foreign ports they will visit and the strange people who will welcome them. The sea is never lonely.'

She must have thought that the moon had gone to my head, and perhaps it had, for it is not often that I can get anyone to listen to my rhapsodizing during the middle watch when things loom bigger than at any other hour of the day. She stared at me rather curiously for a moment, and then fetched me back to earth, and good sound solid earth at that.

'I like bands and lots of people.'

The youth had been revenged.

At that moment Coxton came aft from the fo'c'sle-head where he had been straining his eyes and ears to the utmost.

'I can't hear a thing, sir. The bell buoy can't be working.'

'Not enough sea to swing the clappers,' I said. 'Better try another cast of the lead.'

He swung the lead in his capable hands and let it fly so that it entered the water with a plop just under our bows. The line ran through his fingers and stopped suddenly. As we passed over the lead he lifted it for a foot, and then dropped it vertically on the bottom. 'Just something better than six fathoms and not much tide with us yet. That doesn't help us much.' It didn't help at

all, merely confirmed our belief that we were still in the Wallet and fairly close
to the edge of the bank. We both stood cupping our ears in an effort at catching that elusive ding or ding dong. There were plenty of sounds coming in
from the fog but not the one we were so anxiously hoping to hear.

'What are you listening for?' asked the girl.

'A bell buoy which ought to be somewhere near us.'

'What does it sound like?' 'Just like any other bell; a bit more mournful
than most, perhaps.'

'Is it very important?'

'Yes! To me it is almost of more importance than anything else in the
world just at present. I shall be late in getting back to duty unless we hear it
soon, and that is a serious matter.'

'Oh! I am so sorry.'

'It's my own fault,' I said. 'I shouldn't have stayed so long in Lowestoft.'

'If you hadn't we might have been sleeping on the beach to-night. There
was nothing else left for us.'

'Then I am glad I stayed whatever comes of it. And I dare say I shall be
able to square things up all right so don't worry about it.'

She slipped her hand into mine for a minute, then I left the almost useless
helm and wandered round the deck, restlessly searching for a more advantageous position. The propagation of sound in fog is notoriously uncertain and
erratic both in volume and direction, making me wonder whether, even if I
did hear the bell buoy, I could make any alteration of course with any certainty
that I was acting correctly. The girl had apparently lost all interest in the proceedings and was seated on the deck, leaning her back against the companion.
She yawned several times and the next time I noticed her she had stretched
herself out and was lying with her head on the hard teak planking. I picked up
a deck cushion and was approaching to offer it to her when she suddenly sat
up, looked wildly around and called out:

'I hear it! I hear it!'

'Hear what?' I questioned.

'The bell buoy!'

I stood with the cushion in my hand, and along with Coxton strained in the direction we thought the buoy ought to be. Nothing could be heard except the melancholy hoot of a steamer in the distance. I thought the child had been asleep and had dreamt it, and said so, but she broke in passionately:

'I wasn't asleep! I tell you I heard it quite distinctly. It was just like a church bell tolling, and it wasn't keeping time either.'

That convinced me. She had never heard a bell buoy in her life, and yet she was giving me a meticulously accurate description of what the sound was like. She dropped her head on the deck again, and jumped up as if she had been stung. 'I heard it again! It's in the deck!'

My ear was glued to the deck in an instant. Sure enough there was the faint sound of a tolling bell, and it was irregular so it could not be a submarine signal from one of the lightships. It could only be the sound of the bell buoy propagated through the water and magnified by the hull of the yacht acting as a sounding board. I jumped up and spoke to Coxton who had his ear to the deck as well. 'It's the bell buoy all right. Drop the lead over the stern.'

'Still six fathoms, sir.'

'Let the line run through your fingers and see how it streams.'

'Right away on our starboard quarter.'

I glanced at the compass. 'That is almost due north. The tide must be carrying us through the Spitway. I'm going to alter course to due south. In for a penny in for a pound. Keep the lead going from the starboard chains.'

I was rigid with excitement and anxiety. Was I suddenly to hear that horrible grating under my keel and feel the ship listing as the tide drove her higher up on the sand? It was difficult to trust my judgment when I heard a lugubrious voice, strongly tinged with warning, from the chains, 'Nine feet, sir.' And a moment later, 'Eight feet, sir.' Only a foot of water under my keel, and I involuntarily braced myself for the impact. Again came that warning voice, but no longer in the tones of the condemned, 'Nine feet, sir.' Nine feet! We must be in the channel; if we weren't we must have gone aground by this time, and instead the water was deepening. There was a shout and Coxton started coiling up his line as he spoke: 'Bell buoy fine on your starboard bow, sir.'

I almost collapsed with relief, and sat down on the deck cushion beside the tiller, shaking. I looked up at the buoy as it loomed ghostly in the spectral light which was a compound of dawn, fog, moonlight and night. It gave a final dong (or was it a ding?) as we passed and were free of the sand at last. Of course as always happens at sea we were no sooner clear of the danger than the fog which had been the cause of all the trouble began to lift, and a little breeze gave perfect control of the ship, while the Swin Middle like a hazy ghost ahead made navigation as easy as falling off a log.

Coxton came aft, stowed away the lead and suggested that he would take her for a bit if I wanted to go below for a spell, but I told him to go below himself, as I would not miss a sunrise on the estuary for anything. He yawned and went off towards the fo'c'sle hatch, and, full of delight, I shouted out to him as he went down the ladder, 'We brought that off all right.' 'Jolly good job too, sir,' was the answer as he disappeared. I sat at the helm and hummed and patted myself with satisfaction. I was kidding myself into believing that what was really an outrageous fluke was the natural result of my wonderful navigation and pilotage. No stranding and hazarding where I was in charge! All the wardroom mess would hear about this—casually, of course. Oh yes! It must be very casually, during the next week or so. And when one of those blinking experts, with that passion for exactitude which they only exercise for the confounding of their friends, would say, 'Lot of luck about that sort of thing!' I would retort: 'Luck be damned! Provided you keep your head and your reckoning there's nothing in it.' And I would produce my carefully cooked log to prove it.

To my everlasting shame and disgrace I had forgotten all about that young woman who had ensconced herself in a snug corner between the dinghy and the saloon skylight, and was out of my direct line of vision as I conned the ship towards the Swin Middle. I was startled to find her obstructing my view of that lightship.

'I think I shall go to bed now.'

'Quite right. You'll want some beauty sleep before I put you ashore in Southend. Good night, or rather, good morning.' I must have said something that had annoyed her, because she turned on me like a little spitfire.

'Don't you forget that it was me who found the bell buoy for you, and the next time I tell you anything you don't need to imagine I'm dreaming.'

She turned and stepped down the companion ladder which was about six feet away from where I sat. But just before the head disappeared it whirled round and spat:

'I know that you think I'm just a baby because I cried the other night, but I could tell you a lot of things you don't know or are ever likely to know.'

I wondered what the devil she was driving at, but did not depart from my invariable rule to let the woman have the last word, so she had it. I was left to enjoy the sunrise by myself. It was a beauty.

By nine o'clock we were anchored off Southend pier, and after breakfast my passengers were put ashore. I insisted on the youth taking a pound with him for their present necessities, and said good-bye to them with rather mixed feelings. Miss Impudence seemed glad to get away, and I supposed she still felt sore about my want of tact in not acknowledging her share in the navigation of the previous night. I had a fair wind and tide back to Chatham, and in the classic service phrase, 'returned to my leave'.

A few weeks afterwards I had a letter from the youth enclosing a money order for the sum I had advanced. There was much flowery language expressing gratitude for what I had done to help them, but he gave very little information, except that the girls had got an engagement in London and wished to be remembered to me. Apparently he had found the expected salvation in Southend since his letter bore quite a good address in that town. Occasionally I wondered whether I would ever run across any of them again, but the world I knew went to bits on 4th August, 1914, and the incident was completely forgotten.

*   *   *

The war had been over for about a year, and tired and seedy from foreign service I had come up to town for medical survey at the Admiralty. I had nothing to do that evening, and the waiter at my hotel insisted that I must see a spectacular show which was all the rage, and to get rid of my thoughts which ran gloomily to prospects of invaliding, I arranged for the only stall I could get—a rotten one near the end in the front row. For those who care for that kind of thing I have no doubt the show had many attractions, chiefly of the gorgeous feminine variety. In one scene a row of gaily clad girls was pirouetting at the front of the stage, and I could not help noticing that the one at the end of the line opposite me had found an admirer nearabouts where I was sitting. I feebly wondered who was the lucky man as she was an attractive looking minx. This nodding and smiling went on every time she appeared, and for some reason made me feel devilish awkward, especially as there were no young men close to my seat, and the old dowagers on either side of me were audibly sniffing.

They had still more to sniff about when one of the programme girls came up to me towards the end of an act and, in anything but a whisper, said that Miss So-and-So would like to speak to me at the end of the act. As there is nothing in my appearance or fortune to render me attractive to stage minxes I told the girl that there must be some mistake as I did not know the lady. But as the lady was on the stage at that moment and still nodding vigorously and smiling in my direction, I gave it up as one of those things no fellow can understand, and meekly followed my guide as soon as the curtain had fallen. At the end of a corridor and outside what, from the cackling going on inside, must have been a common dressing-room I found the lady waiting for me. The minute she saw me she rushed forward and seized me with both hands. 'Oh! I am so glad I happened to see you. Just fancy if you had been here and I had not recognized you in time to send you a message.' I was just on the point of saying that she must have mistaken me for someone else when she saw from my expression that I had failed to recognize her. 'How silly of me! Of course, you don't remember me for I've grown up; but you are just the same; I would have recognized you anywhere. Don't you remember the bell buoy?'

That long-lost happy world came back with a rush, and for a second it was a misty morning in the Thames and Miss Impudence was telling me things for the good of my soul.

'My dear, my dear,' I said. 'I am glad to see you again. Tell me about everything.'

Even then the call boy was shouting and there were only a few minutes left, but there was not so much to tell after all. The youth had joined up as soon as the war broke out and had been killed in action. I am sure he was the hero to the end and had died nobly. Her sister had married an officer during the war, and had been made a widow after a fortnight of bliss. She herself was engaged to be married to a man who was very well off, and the wedding was to take place as soon as the show had finished its run. She blushed even through her make up as she said shyly, 'I liked him from the first because he reminded me of you.'

We met again when we had supper at the expense of a tall handsome man with whom I had much in common as he had served in the Navy during the war. But I am still wondering wherein lay the likeness between us which the girl had noted.

XIV

A Bristol Channel Pilot Cutter

FOR YEARS I HAD ARGUED against the conversion of these pilot cutters into yachts, and had declared over and over again that nothing could induce me to indulge in such an expensive and foolish pastime. In my opinion conversion was a mug's game; you poured good money into a worn-out hull, designed and built for a totally different purpose, and, no matter how much it cost or how well the work was done, you might consider yourself lucky if, when the time came to sell, you recovered the cost of the bare hull. The man who agreed to buy from you would, to a certainty, consider that you had made a mess of the alterations, would violently disagree that anything you had done had increased the value of the vessel, and state that you had only added to the cost of the alterations he intended to put in hand without delay. He was almost certain to wind up with an exclamation that he could not live in a boat like this, thereby implying that your standards were so far below his own that he could hardly bear to argue with such a creature. 'Fools build boats for wise men to buy.'

In condonation of my present backsliding from this attitude I must explain that I had just come back from China in the year 1919, invalided, and as shaky as could be, both physically and mentally. All my life the cure for my ailments has been the same, and I considered it essential that I should get to sea for a spell, and see what effect that had on the dysentery that was pulling me to pieces. Also, I wanted to know what it was like to be at sea with only its friendly perils to contend with, free from the horrors with which the devilish ingenuity of man had strewn it during the war. Four years of treading gingerly at sea, wondering each moment whether you were to meet or make some new tragedy, made yachting in peace time a new form of adventure. You could go where you pleased subject to the off-chance of stumbling on a mined area which had not yet been cleared. Appreciated above everything else was the fact that you need no longer darken ship at nightfall, and all the little coastwise winking lights were shedding their rays to welcome you back. In these present days it is difficult to realize all that was meant by the freedom of the seas which had been returned to us after so many years of deprivation.

I tried my best to find a suitable ship, but most of our best yachts had been sold abroad at breakup prices during the war. Other enterprising gentlemen nearer home had bought up the rest with the idea of making a corner, and had succeeded so well that prices had soared enormously, and rotten old wrecks were fetching something better than their building prices at the time of their construction. I did find one yacht that was in fair condition, and offered more than twice her value in order to make sure of getting her, but I was beaten at the post by a war profiteer (a war profiteer was anyone who had more money than I could raise), who at once laid down more than three times her value and took the ship. Years after he told me that it was the most expensive speculation he had ever indulged in, but it was worth it as he thereby gained two years' sailing that would have been otherwise denied him.

After this failure I went to the building yards to see what I could get in the way of new construction. One well-known builder was quite frank. If I had endless money and endless patience he might be able sometime to let me have a boat but he was not to be tied to price or date of delivery. He showed me one small sailing boat, about twenty feet long, whose materials and construction were far below the firm's usual high standard of workmanship, and told me that it had cost the owner £900, his own profit on the transaction being negligible. Other yards had the same story to tell; materials were hard to come by and fearfully expensive while labour had forgotten how to do an honest day's work, had fantastic notions as to its value, and refused to be bound by hours or urgency.

Thoroughly disheartened, I had almost made up my mind that until prices became more reasonable I would just have to do without a boat, and was listlessly reading the advertisements in a yachting paper when I happened on one that was new to me and had not been investigated. In it I read that a pilot cutter, the *Maud*, was for sale at a price only a little above her building cost. Though I did not know the vessel I had heard the name of her owner, well spoken of as a man who had a reputation for seamanship and square dealing, and it struck me that it might be worth while making a visit to Newport where she was lying. After some correspondence I was met by Mr. Adams at the railway station, and he took me to the docks where the *Maud* was lying, in company with some forty discarded vessels of her class. As we approached the derelict group one of them caught my eye, standing out like a queen amongst a beggarly rabble. It was not until I was on her deck that I recognized that, subconsciously, I had already decided if she were not the ship I had come to see there was not the faintest chance of my making an offer for any of the others. On examination I was sorry, as I had never heard of her builders, to find that she had not been built by any of the famous Bristol Channel firms but by a south coast yard and that, as she was built of soft wood, she was already showing slight signs of nailsickness although only about eleven years old.

After a fairly thorough inspection nothing else of importance was found wrong, and the pilot assured me that as far as he knew she was sound and good everywhere. On my asking whether she was reasonably fast he claimed that she was the fastest boat in Newport, and later in the pilot's sitting-room I was shown several silver cups which she had won in the local regattas. On my telling a cynical friend about the cups he said he knew all about them; they were collected from the various owners and temporarily deposited in the house of a seller when a prospective purchaser was expected. In justice to Mr. Adams I must say in later years, when she had passed from my hands under the name of *Saladin*, the *Maud* successfully competed in the Fastnet race and upheld her reputation as one of the fastest working boats that had ever been converted into a yacht.

After a yarn with the pilot I made up my mind to buy the ship, and mentally resolved that I would not spend a single penny on her beyond what was necessary for decent upkeep. She was a rough pilot boat and, as far as I was concerned, she would be kept exactly like one, and there would be no expensive yachting fripperies wasted on her. If ever I could afford a real yacht I would buy one and keep her as such, but until then I would save on every one of the gew-gaws so dear to the heart of the yachtsman and so ruinous to his pocket. If the ship as she was had been good enough for the pilots she was good enough for me—tar and tanned sails was to be my motto henceforth, or so I thought.

The result of this thinking may as well be confessed at once. Within a year I had spent nearly £1000 on her. Her next purchaser allowed me about £250 of this expenditure, chiefly for equipment. As far as the conversion went he considered me a demented idiot in the way I had spoiled a good ship.

After a short discussion with the pilot the price was agreed upon, and arrangements were made for taking her over. I promised to come back on the Wednesday afternoon, and asked that the ship might be ready for sailing at once, on the evening ebb, as I had little time to spare and must get back with as little delay as possible. Mr. Adams thought he could manage to find me two good hands for the trip round to Southampton, and he also arranged for the ship to be put on the slip for survey and coating of her bottom with antifouling, to be done at my expense. When I did turn up at the appointed time I found the ship still on the grid, and was met by the surveyor, a local shipwright, who presented me with a bill for the survey and a report on the ship's condition which I discovered later to be more eulogistic than accurate.

Everything seemed to be going on perfectly until the pilot apologized for being unable to induce the men he had expected to make the trip. I had counted on those men on account of my own physical weakness, and when he told me that, in spite of the very handsome terms I was offering, the only volunteer was an old man of seventy-three whose usual employment was that of ship's caretaker, I felt inclined to throw up the whole business and make other arrangements for her removal. When the old man, Jim, came to see me I liked him, and as there was no chance of any other help we arranged to sail as soon as the ship floated. The worst snag was that I had no charts with me, having expected to be able to buy what I wanted in the town, but desperate hunting failed to bring any to light. The old man said he did not mind as he knew every

Saladin (ex *Maud*) sailing in the Fastnet Race

foot of the Bristol Channel as far as the Lizard if I could do the rest, which I thought was within my powers.

Whilst waiting for the tide to float us the time was filled up by the local pilots coming on board to say good-bye to another old friend. They came into the saloon and sat solemnly on a settee in lugubrious silence, rarely making a remark aside in a sibilant whisper. When the tension became unendurable one would suddenly get up, seize a tumbler from the rack on the bulkhead above the watertank, turn on the tap and half fill the glass. Then looking round and, as I felt, reproachfully at me they all delivered themselves of the same formula: 'Well, that's the old *Maud*. She was a good boat.' The water would be solemnly drunk, and then they shook hands with me and departed to make room for a fresh crowd. At least a dozen of them must have performed this rite, and at the end it was getting on my nerves. With the important exceptions that at their own desire the fluid consumed was both weaker and cheaper, and there was no corpse, the ceremony bore a striking resemblance to the 'coffining' in a bereaved Scottish household. While this was going on stores of all descriptions were tumbling on board, and I am sure from their expressions that the sight of the blankets I had been compelled to buy locally confirmed their impression that the best days of the *Maud* belonged to history.

As evening fell we dropped down the river on the first of the ebb. There was not a breath of wind, and sailing was out of the question, so as she drifted we manned the Spanish burton and hoisted the dinghy on deck. By the time this was secured in the chocks we had received our final funeral oration from the stationary pilot boat at the mouth of the river, and had entered the estuary. Before dark I discovered we had no sidelights, but Jim hoisted the pilot lamp to the spur at the masthead, and in this disguise of a pilot boat on her station the tide carried us rapidly towards Barry Roads, which were crowded with shipping. As we neared the roads preparations were made to let go the anchor since, in the absence of wind, we had very little control over the ship, and an effort at sheering her to seaward had been attended with little success. Jim had warned me that it was a common occurrence for vessels to be carried by the force of the tide across the bows of an anchored ship and sunk. We were lucky and managed to keep clear, but it was anxious work while it lasted.

The night drew on, and as the Nash was showing up well I suggested that I should keep the middle watch. I did not feel like sleeping as I had dozed in the train on the way down, but Jim said that he never could sleep the first night out. It was not necessary for both of us to be on deck so I went below to overhaul the stores. There was no intention of putting in anywhere this side of Southampton, and I found, except for the possibility of having to fall back on ship's biscuit in place of bread, there was plenty of food for a week at least. Before going on deck I went to put some coal on the stove. The coal was kept as usual in the lockers under the seats in the fo'c'sle, and it was plain that my orders to have the bunkers filled had not been attended to as there was barely enough fuel for three days. This was annoying as we had no other means of heating or cooking, and I felt angry with myself that I had not seen to this before leaving. Yachting teaches you that if anything goes wrong the man in charge must take the onus. It is no use trying to put the blame on underlings. When I spoke to Jim about it he said he knew of the shortage but meant to ask the first ship that passed near to let us have some, as was the usual custom of the pilots. This was much easier and cheaper than dragging coal to the ship's berth in dock. It sounded rather astonishing, and I could hardly believe that a big ship would stop just to let us have a little coal, especially as the cutter was no longer a pilot boat. Jim asserted positively that any ship large or small would stop at once, and in the end I found he was right. Before we passed Lundy we had all the coal we could stow, and some fresh bread as well. In fact, they only stopped giving because I would not allow Jim to ask for anything except necessities.

For the next forty-eight hours we drifted about in the Channel, gaining a more than nodding acquaintanceship with the Bull and the Foreland, and all the little villages with their rotten harbours on the north coast of Devon. It is a strange freak of nature that in all that coast there is not a single harbour of refuge that can bear comparison with the perfect ones scattered in such profusion along the south coast. The only shelter for a deep draught ship is under the lee of Lundy, and it was in the dark hours of the third night out that I picked up the lights on the north and south ends of that island. When Jim relieved for the morning watch I remained on deck watching them lose their stabbing intensity in the growing light of a new day. Jim was watching them too, and dreaming of the days when he had looked on Lundy almost as his home port. Suddenly he turned to me: 'You're in the Navy, aren't you, sir?'

'Yes. Why?'

'Did ever you hear about the *Montagu* being wrecked on Lundy?'

No one who had been more than the proverbial dog watch in the Service could fail to know something about this disaster, the most important, as far as the loss of material was concerned, since the *Howe* had stranded in Ferrol. I said as much and then he told me that he was the last man to see the ship before she piled up.

His story was an interesting one. On the night of the wreck he had been on board a pilot boat, and as there was a dense fog they had been keeping in close touch with Lundy and were certain of their position to within a quarter of a mile. During his watch he was astonished to see a large man of war loom out of the fog and steer to pass quite close to the cutter, as if they had been able to see the pilot light at the masthead in a thinner stratum of fog long before the hull was visible. Their engines were stopped, and as they passed the cutter a voice hailed from the bridge and asked whether the pilot could give them the bearing and distance of Hartland point. This was given them at once perfectly correctly. The voice queried the answer and told the cutter she must be wrong, and that they must have lost their bearings. Jim was annoyed at this reflection on his knowledge of his home waters and, as the man-of-war went ahead on his engines, shouted out so that he was certain he must have been heard: 'If you carry on the same course you are on now you will be on the Shutters in ten minutes.' There was some reply which Jim did not catch as the distance was rapidly increasing, but in a little they heard noises that all too clearly indicated the ship was ashore. He had much to tell me of the salvage of the ship, but I only remembered the tragedy of the Court-martial whose verdict and sentence had removed from the Service one of the finest brains that had ever brought scientific lustre to the Navy. There was some confirmation of Jim's story in the fact brought out at the trial, that, when the ship struck, the responsible officers on board thought they were on the rocks off Hartland.

Early in the morning in company with the hundred years old trading ketch *Ceres* we were negotiating the channel between Lundy and Hartland. A fresh westerly breeze was blowing, and the wind was against tide. I was delighted to see how much better weather we were making than the bigger trader which, in these racy waters, had a miserable time of it until she got clear. We very soon dropped her. Then slowly against, and quickly with, the tide we beat to windward past Trevose Head with its off-lying islands, and at dusk picked up the four flashes of Pendeen. But it was late the next evening before, surrounded by French crabbers, we shaved past the Longships, close-hauled on the starboard tack in a freshening south-westerly wind. Nearing the Runnelstone it was evident that if we wanted to weather the rocks we must go about and stand out to sea. I intended to do so as I had no charts or sailing directions, and did not feel that I dared attempt the inside passage with only a doubtful memory of the significance of the beacons on the cliff on shore. But Jim insisted that he knew the passage as well as he knew the palm of his hand and, as the alternative meant an hour's dusting, I allowed myself to be persuaded, although there were many misgivings. Once the die was cast there was no retreat. I need not have worried, as all the rocks under water were marked by wrecks, wartime relics of the nights when the coastwise lights were extinguished. The channel inside was plenty wide enough for anyone, and Jim assured me that big sailing coasters used the passage regularly, and that you could stand inshore until it was possible to throw a lump of coal ashore without coming to any harm.

The weather had completely altered in character since leaving the Bristol Channel, and, instead of the annoying calms and light airs which so far had made the voyage so tedious, we were evidently in for something pretty fierce as the ship raced across Mount's Bay towards the Lizard. While there was still light enough we rolled up four rolls in the mainsail, reefed the staysail, and shifted the working jib for the spitfire. Under this shortened canvas she ought to be able to stand up to anything that might come along. This job had hardly been finished when we dashed through the race off the Lizard, an experience I was anxious to avoid. But Jim did not believe that, apart from Portland, there were any races worth mentioning in the English Channel. They were mere flea-bites compared with the everyday broken waters of the Bristol Channel. I know from my own experience that he was right, but we would have been saved much water on the deck and in the well if we had gone a couple of miles outside the race.

By this time the weather was very threatening, and we discussed whether it would be wiser to put into Falmouth, but my elderly hand was anxious to get the trip over, and I had some curiosity to learn how the ship would behave. At the moment all I could say was that the weather was beastly and looked like being worse, but how much worse there was no way of telling as the barometer was out of action, and there were no wireless forecasts to send you shivering into port, to rant about depressions which, as often as not, are chiefly mental ones. We finally justified carrying on by saying that we would be fools to waste a fair wind and a strong one at that, and that we were having perfect luck after the delays of the last four days. It is extraordinary that as soon as you have decided on a course of action, no matter how rash it may seem, one settles down quite happily to get on with it. It is indecision that frets one's nerves.

Having reached agreement I went below to have a cup of hot tea and a short sleep before I took the middle watch. The fo'c'sle was as snug and warm as could be, and the running motion so easy and comfortable, while the silence was so profound, that I found it difficult to believe that we were out in the Channel in something more than a yachtsman's gale, and that a fairly big ship had to be handled by only two men, one of whom was an invalid, and the other was well beyond the allotted span. I slept like a top and was wakened for relief at midnight. There was no need to ask whether there was any improvement in the weather since the rise and fall of the ship told me that a mountainous sea was running. Jim gave me a dose of cold comfort as he reported: 'Blowing harder than ever but she's running nice and easy. We'd better take in another couple of rolls when you come on deck. There's a lot of fine rain about.' He chuckled when I told him I did not like the look of his face, but I was not long in joining him in the well, where I slacked away the main halliard while he rolled up the reef. When he was finished he went below and left me to take stock of the situation. It was none too pleasant.

A hard south-westerly gale was blowing with occasional squalls of rain. The visibility ranged, as near as I could guess, from a mile to a hundred yards when a rain squall was on, though in the worst of these I was unable to see the length of the ship. By the lights there was a lot of traffic about, but we seemed to be outside most of it, which was a real comfort. The seas were enormous but the ship was running easily with the sheet pinned in, the peak dropped, and the boom topped up to keep it clear of the curling crests. Even in the strong wind it was hardly necessary to use the helm at all, and she would run for a long time without attention until a breaking sea knocked her off her course. Whatever faults the pilot cutters might have had, they had two very real virtues—they could run until all was blue and they could heave-to like ducks.

The watch had been gone about an hour when the storm increased considerably in violence until it was blowing harder than I have at any other time experienced in a small ship. The sea changed its character and became irregular, and the expected happened when a crest broke over our starboard quarter. There was not a lot of vice in it, but it soused me pretty thoroughly, filled one seaboot, and left more water in the well than I cared for. Not for the first time it seemed that the self-draining scuppers took a long time to empty the well. There was nothing for it but to see that this kind of accident did not happen too frequently, so I nursed her all I could, eyeing suspiciously all the big combers as they mounted on the quarter. Perhaps I did save her from some of the worst of them, but if you oppose a low hull travelling at eight knots to a big sea following you at twenty-eight knots an occasional blow is bound to result, and a forty miles an hour wind does the rest with an efficiency that leaves no room for criticism. At first I did not mind the discomfort very much; it was only what must be expected during a hard run, and it was a thrilling experience that I would not have missed for anything. The real truth was that I was not in a fit state to stand a great deal of exposure.

A few months earlier I had been invalided home from China because as the board brutally put it: 'We've already got three of your cloth in the cemetery here, and we don't want any more of you.' Oilskins and seaboots are no protection against breaking seas, and soon I was drenched from head to foot while my feet squelched in my boots every time I moved. Worst hardship of all, I became wretchedly cold and shivered constantly. I had no intention of routing the old man out before the watch was up as he was pretty well worn-out by the watch and watch of the last four days, and could only carry on if he got his fair share of sleep.

To make the time pass I tried a favourite dodge of mine, and thought of all the pickles I had been in; the idea being to take comfort in my present distresses by the remembrance of past difficulties overcome. I can never recollect that the land has caused me any trouble, beyond its failure to provide me with an abiding habitation, but there were quite a few spots of bother at sea that came back with startling exactitude. Hove-to in a gale of wind off Cape Leeuwin with half our boats gone, and watching the clipper ship *Carlisle Castle* drive past at sixteen knots to her doom on the rocks outside Freemantle; caught in a hurricane in the Gulf Stream on board a 250-ton barquentine with the skipper and mate smashing the bulwarks with a sledge hammer to free the deck of water; being driven down on the Sand Islands to the north of Formosa during a typhoon, and wondering whether we were going to repeat the tragedy of the *Bokhara*; all the risks of thirty years of wandering up and down the Seven Seas. I could remember danger in plenty and, in retrospect, could not call to mind that any of it had worried me overmuch. And yet here I was, in no danger at all, maddeningly anxious to get shelter at any cost as long as I could get some respite from this cold and wet. It was easy to talk to myself and call myself all sorts of names, but I shivered just the same. The whole thing was absurd, and I kept telling myself I was absurd, but it did not make the slightest impression on my craving for warmth and shelter.

Away ahead of me I could see the green light of a sailing vessel, and from the irregularity of her course as she came up and fell off I knew that she was hove-to on the starboard tack, so I kept away a little so as to give her plenty of sea room. When we did pass it was near enough to see that she was a big trawler, and she was digging her nose well into the seas. She gave me an idea. Why not heave-to also, go below and sit in front of the fire in the fo'c'sle, get off all my wet things, rub down with a Turkish towel, dress in warm dry clothing, and then sit and drink hot cocoa until the clouds rolled by? It was the sweetest dream I have ever dreamt, and I luxuriated in the details of it. But I could not, without considerable risk to the gear, heave her to by myself, and she would not lay unless the mainsheet was got in, which was too heavy a job for one hand. I must call my hand and tell him what I proposed to do.

In order to leave the deck with some degree of safety it was important to trim the helm so that she would run for a long time without attention or only come up in the wind a little bit. Then I watched my chance and went below to the fo'c'sle, where Jim was telling the world that he was fast asleep. The fo'c'sle looked the most desirable spot in the world. The stove was red-hot from the strong draught in the chimney, and a kettle of boiling water was hissing on the hotplate. Hardly a sound of the fury on deck was to be heard in its warm snugness. The brilliant lamp showed it as the perfect haven of rest for a tired man. All this was taken in at a glance as I leant into Jim's bunk and shook him gently. Like all seamen, he was wide awake at once and in full possession of all his faculties. 'Is it four o'clock?' he asked. 'No!' I said. 'It's not quite three yet.'

He waited for me to explain, and suddenly I knew myself as a miserable funk who had committed the unforgivable sin of waking a man before his watch was due.

'It's blowing very hard on deck,' I mumbled.

He pushed one ear against the wooden ceiling for a moment. 'Yes. It's blowing real hard.'

'Don't you think we ought to do something?' I suggested, weakly hoping that the great idea would present itself to him unaided by anything I might say.

There was no help from him. 'What was you thinking of doing, sir?'

'I was thinking perhaps we'd better heave-to.'

So that was why I had interfered with his sleep. This was easily settled. 'You don't heave-to in them ships unless you are waiting for something.' He turned over on his side and composed himself to sleep again.

I seized hold of a mug of hot water and stole out of the fo'c'sle back to the welter on deck, thanking Heaven that Jim had not spotted the funk I was in, but thought I wanted to consult him on a question of seamanship. When I thought of the fool I had made of myself it kept me hot for the rest of the watch.

When I turned over to him at four I had to tell him that I had not the faint-est idea where I was, as I had been trusting to fix our position by the Eddy-stone but, although we must have passed a few miles south of it, and I had watched most carefully, the squalls of rain had prevented it from showing up. The reply was characteristic: 'Give me deep water on a night like this. I'll keep her to the south'ard.' In less than ten minutes I was asleep, warm and snug in a dry bunk. There is nothing better in all this wide world, but you have to go through the preliminaries of a middle watch in the wind and the rain before you can appreciate these luxuries to the full.

At seven I got up and cooked breakfast, ate mine, and was ready to relieve the deck at eight. The wind was less, and all the indications were that the blow was over although it was very thick. After getting more sail on her I said that I would stand in and pick up the land while Jim went off to feed and clear up. An hour later he pushed his head out of the hatch and asked: 'You haven't got any cows about in these parts, have you?'

'Well, we must be pretty near Devon, and they think a lot of their cows in that part of England. Why?'

'I thought I heard one of them mooing just now.'

I listened carefully. Our exact position was doubtful, and cows, gulls, dogs, and cockerels have saved many a ship from stranding in thick weather. Then far away on the port bow was heard the dismal wail of a fog siren. We timed it and in a minute it was repeated.

'That's the Start. Now we have some idea where we are.'

At five that afternoon we had Portland Bill abeam, twenty-two hours from the Longships, but the adverse tide and a failing wind made us miss our tide at the Needles. For nearly four hours we barely held our position between the south-west shingles and Bridge buoy. Then as the tide eased we sailed up the Solent in the rays of an early morning sun, and anchored off the Royal Pier at Southampton, five days and ten hours out of Newport. The last insult was when the skipper of a tug which I wanted to tow me up to Eling came alongside in response to my hail and asked whether anybody on board could speak English. He explained afterwards that he had mistaken us for a French crabber.

XV

'Freda'

THE SOUTH-WEST WIND WAS LIGHT, and without auxiliary power progress was painfully slow as we beat down from the Bag to the entrance of Salcombe harbour. 'That's a fine powerful sea-going craft you have got there,' was shouted to me by an elderly man in a half-decked sailing boat as he passed. 'She is all that,' was my answer, although my disloyal preferences at the moment were all for considerable sacrifice of sea-going power for the sake of a little more speed in light airs. At our present rate of progress the ebb would be running hard by the time the bar was reached and, as the run in on the previous ebb had warned me, there would be some highly unpleasant rollers to be negotiated before we could reach the comparative comfort of the turbulent waters round the Prawle and Start. Although it was the middle of July the weather was all out of joint and was more like that usually associated with Cowes week—in fact we had been sheltering securely in the recesses of Salcombe from a two days' southerly gale, when our real objective was Exmouth, where a friend had promised to kill the fatted calf to celebrate our arrival. But not even the owners of thirty-five-ton pilot cutters are rash enough to attempt the estuary of the Exe in an on-shore gale.

The wind had died away completely but the ebb was beginning to take charge, and hurrying us towards the Blackstone beacon. The skipper, who had been attending to the head sheets forward, saw what was coming to him by the seas breaking over the partially submerged rocks, and the frantic appearances and disappearances of the Wolf Rock buoy beyond. Hastily he brought the fore and jib sheets to the cleats on the cockpit coaming, chucked all the halliard falls into the dinghy, pulled the fo'c'sle slide over the hatch, adjusted the hatch cover, and then, with an enforced step and dance which fully justified the precautions he had been making, joined me in the cockpit. Like all pilot cutters' wells, this was deep enough to ensure that at least we could not be thrown out of it. After hardening in the mainsheet to control the now useless boom he turned to me with a grin and, 'Going to get it in the neck,' he suggested.

But it wasn't so bad after all. The greatest danger was the complete lack of control which at one moment allowed the tide to carry us perilously near the rocks and, a little later, prevented us from crossing the bar in the best water. There was the usual series of violently rapid dives into a crested array of steep rollers; the usual submersion of the bowsprit and fo'c'sle head right up to the mast; the usual thunder of water aft along the deck; the usual crashes from below, where an insecurely fastened door and an overlooked earthenware bowl were chanting their several paeans of unfettered freedom; the usual moment of sickening anxiety as she fell to the bottom of an extra deep trough and one wondered whether, thus far out of the channel, there was enough water for her nine feet of draught; and then, as suddenly as we had entered the hurly burly, it was all over. We stood out to sea on the starboard tack, rising and falling to a huge swell which was more seen than felt on board our craft, though it was breaking in cataracts of foam over the bows of a big cargo steamer as it forced its hideous mass to the westward.

The one snag about leaving Salcombe bound east is that, in a purely sailing vessel, the prevailing westerly winds and the depths of water forbid departure except during the ebb. Consequently you may be held up by a foul tide round the Prawle and the Start—headlands which are not conspicuous for the quietude and serenity of their surrounding waters. In the light south-easterly air which had sprung up there was nothing to be gained by attempting a direct route, so much physical discomfort was avoided by plying to the southward for the few hours that must elapse before the uncertain tide could be presumed to have turned in our favour. The breeze, fitful and declining, finally petered out altogether, and at sunset left us becalmed on a glassy sea three miles east of Berry Head. There was nothing for it but a night out.

Personally, I have never objected to a night out as long as I am doing something or getting somewhere, but to keep a night watch just in case something may happen is unspeakably boring. And nothing did happen, so that when I sat down to breakfast at eight o'clock next morning a glimpse of Berry Head through the thick haze showed me that it bore due west, estimated distance three miles. Except for the tide which had carried us round in a gentle ellipse we had not advanced a foot. Life on board was pleasant enough; my skipper and I had a reasonable amount of sleep undisturbed by the motion of the ship or the necessity for action; meals well cooked and appetizing had appeared at their appropriate intervals, and I had had a bath and a shave before breakfast—the greatest of all luxuries on board a small cruiser at sea. But we were not any nearer Exmouth.

About eleven in the morning a light air from the south-east sprang up, and course was shaped for the Exmouth bar buoy. The weather was thicker, visibility not much better than a mile, and the sky overhead was obscured. The glass, which had recovered from the recent blow, was perfectly steady, and all appearances pointed to a spell of fine, settled, summer weather. By three o'clock land was seen on our port bow and, after careful scrutiny on account of the haze, was recognized as the high land to the west of the Warren. Now the wind died away completely, and the tide swept us along the shore towards Dawlish, at the same time making us close with the beach. This tendency to drive ashore became so marked just off the Parson and Clerk that the anchor was let go and fifteen fathoms of cable veered in four fathoms of water.

It is well known to all coasters that a very light easterly breeze can raise a most annoying popple of a sea in all the bights on the south coast, and this popple had become more and more evident as we drifted along the coast. The motion it imparted had shaken all the wind out of the canvas. Now with her foresail and jib stowed the ship rode to her anchor head on to the swell, which was rapidly increasing and beginning to break. I had delayed too long in letting go, and we were in water too shallow not to affect the sea.

In such a position, and doubtful whether this abominable swell might not portend some rapidly approaching gale from the south-east, I hailed a large motor launch, crowded with passengers, which was passing on its way from Exmouth to Torquay. As the launch drew near a female figure, staunchly supported on either beam by masculine admirers, waved joyous greetings to me which, in other circumstances, I might have felt inclined to acknowledge. Instead I addressed myself to the skipper and asked him whether he would tow me into Exmouth. Before the import of my message had penetrated to his dull wits I found that I had converted the waving lady into a little virago. 'He'll do nothing of the kind,' she shouted. 'We're going on a trip to Torquay and we're not going to have it spoiled for you or anybody like you.' Evidently closer inspection had failed to confirm her first generous estimate of my attractions, and the rest of my conversation with the skipper was punctuated with acid comments on myself, my skipper, my yacht, and, above everything else, my superlative cheek. The latter quality—a mental not a physical attribute I gathered—she confessed to the whole world she liked and admired intensely, but friendliness on the strength of this sole redeeming feature of mine seemed unlikely. The skipper told me he could only deviate from his voyage to assist a vessel in distress. I hastily assured him that I was not in distress, only bored with the calm, and anxious to save my tide into Exmouth. He said in that case he could not help me, and pushed off to the accompaniment of a final spate of compliments from my lady admirer.

Evening was about to fall when the tide turned and began to run to the east. With the change in the tide the rotten sea which had been troubling us all the afternoon rapidly subsided. Hoping that if I got away on the port tack with a weather-going tide under my lee bow the faint air from the south-east might drag me away from my dangerous proximity to the land, the headsails were hoisted and the anchor weighed. The result was as we hoped, and inch by inch we dragged into deeper water. But it was fearfully slow work, and our hopes of getting into harbour before high water about three a.m. were rapidly disappearing when I hailed a passing motor fishing boat and again asked for a tow into Exmouth. His reply was that he was not going to lose a night's fishing for any tow. I said that the tow could not possibly take more than two hours, and I was prepared to pay him three pounds for the service. This made

Deck view of *Freda* looking forward

his mates in the boat start arguing with him, but he repeated that that sum was not worth his while. I then asked him what was worth his while, but he refused to answer this question and shoved off. I heard afterwards that his refusal to tow was because the authorities in Exmouth had a short and sharp way with unlicensed pilots.

Apparently we were booked for another night out so the watches were set, the skipper keeping what remained of the first while I turned in all standing on the saloon settee so as to be ready for the middle. Before I went below we put the ship about so that she was heading east on the starboard tack. At that time our estimated position was about a mile to the east of the Orestone. Visibility was limited to a radius of half a mile, but there was nothing in sight.

After a hot drink I took on at midnight. There was nothing to report; we were still on the same tack, the ship was making a knot or less through the water, which was absolutely smooth; visibility was much the same, but it was clearing overhead and a few stars were to be seen in the zenith; there was a deathly stillness which compelled us to converse in whispers. I guessed our position as about eight miles from the bar buoy and gave up all hope of being able to enter the Exe until after midday—if then. The skipper went and turned in, and I was left to while away the four hours' watch as best I could. As we had undoubtedly missed our tide there was no hurry and everything was peacefully pleasant. Close-hauled the ship could look after herself better than she could be steered, so I left her to her own devices with perfect confidence whilst I, somnolently, kept such a look-out as I considered necessary in the little-frequented waters between Berry Head and Straight Point.

As the time went past, the motion of the ship was barely perceptible. The sky was still clearing overhead, but there were no signs of the coast and the horizon became contracted by a luminous pale blue mist, the precise colour and consistency of which I had never seen in English waters, though they had been unpleasantly familiar as the precursors of a hurricane in the tropics. But the glass remained steady, and there was nothing else to account for the foreboding that seemed to come from nowhere and engulfed me. The coke stove was always kept going at sea with a kettle of water on top of it, so, towards the end of my watch, I went below to make a cup of tea before calling my relief.

Coming on deck while waiting for the kettle to boil I gave the usual glance at the ship, the sea and the sky. The latter arrested my attention at once. The stars had disappeared overhead, the luminous mist had been swept away, and far off on the port bow could be seen the twinkling lights of a town, readily recognized as Dawlish by the two green lights standing brilliantly out against the background of white sparklers. I had just noted the extraordinary brightness of the lights and was wondering why they should be associated with a horrible feeling of depression when my attention was distracted from them by a deepening of the gloom in the sky, and there, on the western horizon, a low pall of jet-black cloud with a horrid-looking opalescent orange-red centre was rapidly mounting and spreading in every direction all over the sky.

I called the skipper at once, and one glance at that ominous cloud was enough for him. In a very few minutes we had the topsail off her and stowed below, and then the headsheets were shifted over in case we were taken aback. We stood for a moment in the well and discussed the question of rolling up a reef while we watched that rapidly mounting horror. I was unwilling to shorten canvas as the ship was snugly rigged and well able to stand up to most weather we were likely to meet. Also I was sick of baffling calms and light airs, and this looked like being a fair wind. Even while we talked, and really before we could have done anything, the angry roar of the wind broke on our ears and, simultaneously, with a crash the boom flew over to the starboard side with a jerk that must have torn the main horse out of the deck if it had not been for the powerful spring buffers with which it was fitted. The vessel lurched over and over to the fury of the squall until the boom and most of the sail was in the water, and she was on her beam ends.

With no way on her and pressed down by the weight of the wind so that the rudder was out of the water, while she was actually being blown sideways over the surface, we could do nothing to help her. Indeed, it was only with the greatest of difficulty we could keep ourselves in the cockpit by standing on the lee coaming and hanging on with both hands to the weather one. The spindrift picked up by the wind was driven in cascades over the weather bulwarks and clean over our heads into the sea beyond. Though in previous cruises I had come through much bad weather in *Freda* I had never imagined her covering board being forced under the water, and now the sea was level with the starboard coamings of the skylights and pouring in over the lee coaming of the well. My skipper shouted to me through the uproar that he was going to let fly the mainsheet, which was made fast to a bollard close to the weather coaming, but I ordered him to leave it alone and to give the ship a chance to recover herself. I feared that if the sheet were started the sail would begin flogging, and very little of that would take the mast over the side. Such a result would have been a disaster, and I was by no means convinced that our predicament was so grave that the risk of disaster must be taken in order to avoid a more imminent and greater peril. All the gear was good, and not likely to carry away now that it had withstood the first impact of the squall.

The ship seemed to have heeled as far as she was likely to go; the ballast was cemented in and could not shift; so far she could not have taken in much water, and she could lie as she was for some time before that became a serious problem. I was of opinion that she could only be forced farther over and made to founder by a fairly big sea striking her on the exposed bilge, and this was not likely as the sea was still smooth and likely to remain so until the weight of the squall had passed. I was positive that as soon as the squall lightened the least little bit she would pick herself up and get going again; as soon as that happened all immediate danger would be over. It sounds a lot to think about when lying on your beam ends, but I can assure any doubter that that position, even at three on a summer's morning, is calculated to hasten one's mental processes amazingly.

In discussing this affair with many well-known cruising men I have received much information as to what I ought to have done. The fact remains that, purposely, nothing was done. After a period of unspeakable tension which appeared to last a long time but was, in all likelihood, only a few minutes by the clock, the wind let up ever so little, but even that little was sufficient to let *Freda* come up and she began to drive ahead instead of sideways.

As soon as the rudder gave control again the tiller was put up to steady her on the course for Straight Point, now clearly visible in the half light of dawn, and away she tore like the proverbial scalded cat. It has almost broken my heart to try and get seven knots out of those Bristol Channel Pilot Cutters of which I have sailed many and owned two, but this was the only occasion when I felt I was driving one at her maximum speed of over nine knots. We ought to have taken in a couple of reefs and shifted jibs, but port was in sight, the ebb had already started, and, if we were to be sure of sufficient depth to carry our nine feet of draught up the channel, there was no time to be lost.

As it was it was doubtful whether, unless the wind freed a little, we could lay up from the bar buoy without tacking. As tacking against a four-knot ebb is hopeless work, it meant dodging about outside for six or eight hours until the flood had made sufficiently. There was the prospect that, at the end of that time, I should find the rising gale had closed the entrance to the harbour, and that I was hopelessly embayed on a lee shore. Neither of us had by any means reached that dangerous state of mind when a decision is taken to make for harbour at any cost, but it was going to take a lot to keep us outside if there were any possibility of nosing our way in. Luckily, as we neared Straight Point, keeping an anxious lookout for the bell-buoy which marks the best water over the bar, the wind was found to be backing until it steadied at south-west. This gave us a fair wind in, but the change brought in a heavier sea which the ebb caused to break right across the bar. It looked pretty awful but did not seem more than was reasonable to attempt, so we put her at it and, not for the first time, found every justification for our trust in these fine sea-going vessels. The strength of the gale may be judged from the fact that our speed over the ground seemed in no way diminished by the ebb running against us.

As we drove up past the Mere and were at last in smooth water, we passed within thirty feet of an old boatman who was busy salvaging some pleasure boats which had broken adrift from their moorings during the night. He stared at us in astonishment as we stormed in from the welter outside. His reaction to my perfectly civil good morning was to stand up unsteadily in his boat, hold both hands stretched out towards heaven, and shriek at the top of his voice, 'You may thank your God you have managed to get in out of that!' My skipper looked at him sourly and replied, 'You go to hell!' It was the only time in seven years together I have known him to show signs of frayed nerves.

Some people may remember the sudden midnight storm that swept over the south country on that summer night in July, 1923. It caused much havoc in the country and serious damage in the towns, London suffering severely. The force of the wind had all sorts of fantastic estimates attached to it. I am not likely to forget the occasion, but I have no idea what the strength of the wind in the squall was. I know that I have been carrying my topsail when *Tern III*, with Dr. Worth on board, was down to two reefs and a small jib, so that a wind that could lay *Freda* on her beam ends must have been pretty fierce. I recognized afterwards that, subconsciously, I had been expecting something of the kind ever since leaving Salcombe. Those who have had any experience of the curious mental state that precedes all tropical storms will understand what I mean.

The distance from Salcombe to Exmouth is about thirty-four miles. We took forty-four hours to do it.

XVI

The Quest in 'Patience'

I T WAS A GREY DULL DAY and raining heavily. Nothing could have looked more unpromising, as far as the weather was concerned, for a single-handed cruise in a twenty-two-ton cutter. But my heart was light as I turned my back on the old life in which I had been the tiniest cog in the smallest wheel of a mighty machine for thirty years, and went gaily down to the jetty where my old friend, and skipper, was waiting for me in the dinghy.

One hundred and sixty-five miles to go, right up the English Channel from Portsmouth until I reached the South Foreland, through the Gull Stream to the North Foreland, and then a dash across the mouth of the Thames, with its multitudinous sandbanks, until I reached Harwich. I could trust to my engine for a little help, but four-knots speed would be of little value in a four-knot tideway, and the tanks only held sufficient fuel for fifty miles at the outside. Luckily the wind, what there was of it, was from the north-west, and to me it seemed to be simply a question of endurance—whether the manpower could stay the distance. Also there was the quest to cheer me up and support me if the winds and tides proved adverse, and the one thing I was convinced of was that no port would see my anchor until I had gained my end.

The tides and courses had all been mapped out and calculated beforehand, and everything that could possibly be foreseen had been taken into consideration and allowed for. It had not encouraged me overmuch to read the account of the passage through the Looe Channel in the *Channel Pilot*, which must surely have been written by the most pessimistic writer of these pessimistic documents: 'The Looe Channel, lying as it does within the whole line of dangers, barred at its narrow western entrance by overfalls, and having in many parts not more than eighteen feet at low water, is only adapted for vessels of

light draught or for those possessing local knowledge except under very favourable circumstances. Great judgment is requisite to avoid being caught
within it at night, and no seaman should take this passage at any time unless
with a good breeze and plenty of daylight before him, nor should a sailing vessel attempt it with an adverse tide.' Well! I proposed going through the Looe!

We slipped from the buoys where my ships had lain for years, and went
down to the jetty under the engine to fill up with water and stores. About 3
p.m. this was completed, and my skipper climbed regretfully from the deck to
the pier above. 'Anything else I can do for you, sir?' he asked, almost wistful-
ly, as he stood looking down on me. And then, suddenly and passionately, as
he remembered the storm and sunshine we had borne during our seven years'
cruising together, he burst forth, 'I wish to God I was coming with you!'

I smiled a bit as I remembered the reasons why it was out of the question. There were six of them, and my first acquaintance with them came one
stormy evening some five miles south of Portland Bill, when we were carrying
all the canvas we could hoist in order, if possible, to save our tide through the
Needles so that I could return 'to my leave'. We had just passed *Tern III* well
reefed down and turning to windward, and that great seaman Worth had sent
us a cheery hail as he passed in a smother of spindrift. As she faded in the
distance my skipper had put his brains to work, and, as the result of his cogitation, came aft to the helm. 'Don't you think we had better get that topsail off
her, sir?' 'Don't talk nonsense! If we take the topsail off her we'll miss our
tide at the Needles.' He went away and lit his pipe, but the overfalls, even five
miles off the Bill, made it impossible to smoke with any degree of pleasure,
and in a little back he came. 'I think I'd better get the topsail off her, sir.' It
was rarely he interfered with the management of the ship, and this time it
annoyed me—partly, I expect, because I knew perfectly well that the topsail
would have to come in soon. 'What the devil is the matter with you, moaning
about the topsail? I'll tell you when the topsail is to come in.' He went off to
do something forward and got well soused in the doing of it, which upset him,
but his next remark had nothing to do with topsails, and yet it brought the
topsail in at once. 'I've a wife and five children in Gosport, sir.' This was too

much for me to stand without laughing. 'Oh! All right! We'll get the damned thing in then.'

When I had asked him to come with me in the new life I was entering upon he had reiterated that he had six good reasons why he dared not become the Ishmael I contemplated, but that did not prevent me from answering him standing dismally on the quay, 'I wish to God you were!'

And then, 'Cast off that line forrard.' He turned to do as he was bid, and a minute later was waving good-bye as I motored down the little creek. Rounding Blockhouse it was time to begin the struggle with the big mainsail, 750 square feet of it. ('We watched you doing it and still we don't know how it was done,' as some amateurs once told me after seeing me leave Weymouth Harbour.) And just beyond the entrance to the harbour, the engine was turned off, the jib unrolled, the staysail hoisted, and the great adventure of a new life had begun.

It has been said of the naval officer that the moment he is free to choose where he will live, the years of subservience to orders from above have so destroyed his initiative, he lies wherever the Admiralty chooses to drop him. If his release comes to him while stationed at Portsmouth he retires to Southsea, but if on the opposite shore of the harbour he buys a house in Alverstoke. Some, greatly daring, do vice versa. If the sentence of old age and its consequent senile dementia comes at Plymouth, there is Mannamead to fall back on with Yelverton in the background for the country lover. I had refused to conform to this routine. Forty years knocking about the Seven Seas had merely accentuated a habit begun in childhood, and the small talk of Service affairs round the bar of the Naval Club from six to seven p.m.—the one hour of the day in which some of my contemporaries captured for a fleeting moment the glamour of the past—savoured too much of the 'has-been' to offer any attraction. I had got a boat and I meant to make that boat my home until such time as the advancing years drove me ashore to await the inevitable end. I was to go wherever the whim of the moment decided and, since no self-respecting hand would tolerate such a vagabond existence, perforce I must travel alone.

I go to sea in *Patience*

It being August Bank Holiday, Southsea beach was crowded with drenched trippers. As it is impossible to work in oilskins I was in no better case. The wind was so light that a small sailing dinghy easily passed me, and my prospects of threading the Looe Channel before dark became gloomy. However, as I passed through the Dolphins marking the passage in the submarine obstruction the wind freshened a little, and, allowing for the strong tide which seemed to be anxious to carry me down to the Nab and round the Owers, a course was laid for the Pullar buoy, S.E. by E. Progress was painfully slow, and it was nearly eight p.m. before the buoy was abeam, and darkness had fallen before the traverse of the Looe passage was accomplished.

As soon as Eastborough Head buoy was well on the starboard quarter, and there was plenty of sea room to dodge about in, I began to think of my own necessities. My clothing was soaked, and that abominable trickle down the back which just reached the waist had begun to annoy. The sidelights had to be got out of their locker, lit and fixed in their screens. Also I wanted something to eat as there had been no opportunity for a meal since breakfast. There was no cockpit in my ship but there was a picnic hamper in the sail-locker aft just under where I sat and steered. Whatever other ships may do, and I read accounts of their docility with much envy and just a little doubt, my ship will not steer herself in a quartering wind unless the sea is flat calm. Here there was just enough swell and popple to divert her from the straight path, and the question of saving tides at Beachy negatived the delay consequent on heaving-to. Still, with much tiller lashing and sudden dives down below, I managed to ship into dry warm clothing, light and screen the sidelights, light the binnacle lamps and get something to eat. By the time all this was finished it was completely dark except for a yellow glare in the western sky where the clouds had cleared sufficiently to show a crescent moon just setting. To port the lights of Bognor and Littlehampton could be recognized, Worthing would soon be abeam, and away ahead on the port bow was a radiance in the sky from the towns of Hove and Brighton. Beachy Head was about twenty-five miles distant, and with the wind at its present strength I had no hopes of carrying the flood round that elusive headland. Luckily the rain had stopped.

'Good God! You don't mean to say you are all alone in that boat!' a friend
had shouted at me when he had passed under his engine one bright spring
morning. The question had come at an unexpected moment, because I had
been so deep in meditation I had not noticed his approach. The morning was
warm and balmy, and I was sitting on the warm deck while the ship bore me
along with a gentle beam wind. My bare feet were the subject of study, and I
had come to the conclusion that God, who had made my feet, knew his job all
right, but the bootmaker, who had made the boots I had been compelled to
wear when a boy at school, had been an ignorant fool. The query took me so
much aback that my friend swore afterwards I jumped up and looked confus-
edly around, and then replied, 'Ye-es, I think so!' I had had no sensation of
being alone that beautiful morning, but now the terror that walks in darkness
had just sufficient hold on me to make me feel very small and lonely when I
looked up at the enormous mass of the mainsail and wondered how I had got
it up and whether I could ever get it down again if a sudden need arose. I knew
that yellow glare meant wind, but mere weight of wind did not cause me any
anxiety as long as it was in the right direction.

Now I was running as the wind had gradually backed to the west, and it
was difficult to keep a good look-out from where I sat aft with my feet dangling
into the sail-room hatch. The ship had been purposely kept inside the main
line of Channel traffic, and far away to starboard could be seen the procession
of rubies, emeralds and topazes which indicated where the big steamers were
passing on their lawful occasions. But others, like myself, who depended on
wind power, had crept into the bight between Beachy and Selsea Bill, and red
and green lights appeared with startling suddenness out of the darkness.

To my mind there is something almost sinister about the sailing ship's
lights at night-time. The steamer's lights look quite cheerful, thanks to her
masthead light, and there is little difficulty in judging the distance and the
direction in which she is travelling, while the noise of the engines and the
beat of the propeller can be heard miles away. But that dim red light on your
starboard bow, which has noiselessly sprung from nowhere and looks so perilously close—what is he, and how is he heading? Your sea sense tells you

it is a ship on the port tack probably a mile or more away. Probably you are right, and there is nothing to get alarmed about, but at least once that night the red suddenly changed to red and green, then back to red, then red and green again, and finally to green. Only a ship going about which has missed stays in the light air, but it seemed to be taking place just under my bows, and I could only have followed out the Rule of the Road and kept out of the way at the expense of a very awkward jibe. Of course there was plenty of room for her to manoeuvre as much as she liked, but it did not look like it. At first I showed her my red light, and then there was a hasty starboarding of my helm to show her my green light, all the time ducking my head in anticipation of the crashing boom—it weighed three hundredweight—as the mainsail took charge. Nothing happened, and she must have been at least half a mile away when I caught the loom of her dark sail against the faint eastern dawn.

About 4 a.m. we were off Newhaven, and the tide had turned against me. Almost fretful with impatience and tiredness, I watched the slowly opening land round the Seven Sisters and guessed that I was not doing more than a knot over the ground. I had hoped to emulate that mythical sailing ship so happily described in the *Sailing Directions*, which, travelling at eight knots, reaches the tidal node eastward of Beachy at high water at Dover, and then carries a fair tide as far as the North Foreland and perhaps even up the Thames. I have never met that lucky ship, but I know, given favourable conditions, my ship is capable of eight knots, though whether I should be perfectly happy while she was doing it there is good reason to doubt. I have known her to approach that speed to my intense discomfort.

Still I struggled on, hoping to get past Beachy some time, with the usual engine problem troubling me. It is not so easily settled as one might think. Briefly it is—Shall I run my engine now and expend fuel which I have no opportunity of replacing, or shall I save my fuel for a real emergency? But at eight a.m. Beachy still refused to come under my stern, and in sheer desperation I turned on the engine, and so got past after running under power for an hour and a half.

There had been a perfect low dawn and the mild westerly wind was slowly backing and freshening. By eleven I was running before a nice south-west breeze, and began to keep a look-out for the Royal Sovereign lightship. By midday it was abeam, and at four in the afternoon Dungeness, the most wicked and desolate of headlands, was passed. The strong breeze was piling up a short curling sea which was very difficult to steer before, especially as I always run with my boom well in and topped up, and the peak halliards slacked a bit so that an unexpected jibe may be robbed of half its terrors. Up to this time I had not felt particularly tired or sleepy, but the added exertion required to keep the ship in front of the sea by means of twiddling lines on the seven-foot tiller was considerable, and twice I woke myself up by sharply rapping my forehead against the end of the tiller. But the haste I was in would not allow me to waste a single moment of that glorious breeze, and I somnolently rejoiced that I had been granted that greatest of a sailor's blessings — a fair wind.

The ship was slipping rapidly along with both wind and tide in her favour. Ahead of me, but inshore, was a big sea-going barge which had been hull-down ahead when I saw her coming out of Rye earlier in the day, and it was evident I was rapidly overhauling her. Now there was another puzzle to solve. If this wind held it was just possible to carry the tide up to the North Foreland and on into Margate Roads, where I could anchor and pass the hours of darkness while waiting for the tide that would carry me across the mouth of the Thames, and catch the young flood into Harwich. My time-table had been all upset by the light winds I had met during the night, and perhaps it would be better to anchor for the night in the harbour of Dover so temptingly under my lee, in case the wind failed and I could not get into Margate Roads. I looked over the ship's side and asked the big comber which was hissing and breaking as it ran along my rail what he thought about it, and as plainly as if gifted with speech he told me, 'If you anchor in Dover you will find me there.' I remembered the times I had rolled and rolled and rolled in that most misbegotten of harbours and decided that I would be more comfortable at sea.

So the barge and I rounded the South Foreland together, and, as I passed under her stern to take my place on her weather quarter, I read her name,

Major, of Harwich. She was bound for the same port as myself, and for a moment it felt as if that harbour were opening to admit me.

The time was 6.15 p.m., and the course led up through the Gull Stream. There was no doubt that the wind, though still fairly fresh, was taking off and still less doubt that at sunset it would die away altogether, and there were still fourteen miles to go before the North Foreland could be left astern and another three miles to the anchorage in Margate Roads.

Here, in smooth water under the lee of the land, the ship was travelling much faster than she could under power. Over the land the sun was quickly sinking as the Gull lightship came abeam and there was promise of fog in the haze which obscured Ramsgate and Broadstairs. Never yet, and I have travelled the route often enough, have I carried a fair wind from the South to the North Foreland; never yet have I managed to catch that fair tide which runs up the Thames for two hours after high water at Dover. Even as I came abreast of the Dike and Quern off Ramsgate the nose of the Gull lightship slowly swung to the north and the breeze died down to fitful patches. Now, if I ever meant to reach Margate Roads, was the time to turn on the engine, and it was the work of but a minute to do so. A bee-line was made for the North Foreland and I trusted to the afterglow to show me the buoy on the Longnose. But long ere I got there and when the Foreland light was just coming abeam, there was a cough and splutter from the engine which I knew heralded trouble, and as I realized this the trouble arrived and the engine stopped. There was no time to investigate; the tide was sweeping me backwards with indecent haste, darkness was coming on rapidly and the wind had completely gone, so I let go the anchor with the lighthouse bearing W by N and distant about two cables. The *Major* had brought up well outside and to the southward of me.

The mainsail was wringing wet with dew and as stiff as pasteboard. Stowing it in these circumstances is the one job I find impossible to do by myself. So I did my usual trick of rolling it round the boom with the patent reefing gear for about the equivalent of three reefs and then bunched the rest until I could get the tiers round and set up. The staysail ran down easily—trust me to have hanks big enough for that—and the Wykeham-Martin gear settled the stowing of the jib. The riding-light was lit and hoisted on the fore-stay, fifteen fathoms of cable were veered, and when this work was completed I knew I could be in no better case for an unexpected emergency during the hours of darkness than if I had a full crew on board.

After knocking about in ships both big and little for over forty years I can honestly say that rolling at anchor hardly affects me at all—in fact I hardly notice it until the ship starts throwing me about. To say that we were rolling violently in the short tidal chop off the North Foreland would be exaggeration, and yet the noises down below were infernal. No small yacht seems really fitted to withstand rolling. Doors on hooks chatter incessantly, locker doors always seem to have a little play and bang to and fro, some jug on a hook in the pantry collides with another jug, the water in the tank under the floor splashes and sounds as if the ship were full of water and about to sink, whilst an angry thud from aloft and conducted below where the cabin acts as a sounding box tells of the impact of a block against the mast.

The noises were left to themselves. There was nothing I could do to stop them and there was much more urgent work to be done anyhow. The picnic basket had been empty since sunrise as my twenty-nine hours at the tiller had given me no opportunity to replenish it, so the first necessity was food. A cup of something hot was prepared and gratefully drunk and some bread and butter eaten. Then the engine was tackled, and the fault, a choked carburettor jet, diagnosed and remedied. By this time it was past midnight and the ship a little quieter, so pulling a coat over me after setting the alarm for three o'clock I lay down on one of the saloon settees and in a trice was dreaming of the end of my adventure.

I woke with a shiver at 4.30 a.m. Dawn was struggling through the skylight, the ship was curiously still, and the alarm was stopped at 12.30. Wrathfully I went on deck and sleepily looked for the North Foreland, which seemed to have been removed overnight. In the pale dawn far to the south of me blinked a light whose period proved that it must be the North Foreland, while to the west of it were land and houses which I guessed, rather than knew, indicated the position of Margate. A steamer lay in the roads, and coming from the direction of the Horse and Gore a barge drifted lazily. Over all the waters brooded a haze and stillness broken only by the cluck of some distant seabird.

Anyone who has anchored on the soft sand which encumbers the estuary of the Thames can guess what had happened. The ship had been slowly towing her anchor through the sand whilst I slept, and, luckily for me, she had dragged it in the right direction. Evidently she also was anxious to reach the end of the adventure. But, as always happens at sea, this dragging and the failure of the alarm clock compelled me to deviate from my pre-arranged programme.

When bound across the mouth of the Thames to Harwich several routes are available, the choice depending on the tide, the wind, the speed desired, and several intangibles such as curiosity, seamanship and pilotage ability. My original idea was to take the last of the ebb up to the Edinburgh lightship and then cross the Barrow Deep and into the Swin by a channel which is deep enough for a small ship close to Knock John. The failing ebb should then allow me to cross the Wallet Spitway and catch the young flood into Harwich. But by 9.30 a.m., when I was off the Edinburgh lightship, the ebb was nearly finished, and to run down so far to leeward of the tide would have made it impossible for me to reach Pin Mill at my appointed time of 2.30 p.m., as I should be against the flood the whole way. There was not a breath of wind, and although my engine was running perfectly I had kept the fuel question constantly in front of me, for there was now only sufficient for six hours' steaming, and my progress past the Edinburgh lightship was so slow on account of the adverse tide that I saw myself hopelessly becalmed and helpless unless I could reach my anchorage before the fuel gave out.

It was a nice fix. Luckily I knew my Thames fairly well and made up my mind to take the ebb down the unbuoyed Black Deep and sail round the head of the Barrow and Gunfleet Sands to the Cork light vessel. There was a little risk in doing this as one ought, in an unbuoyed channel, to have the lead going constantly, and attention to the tiller made this extremely difficult. But just as I entered the Black Deep I saw a Conservancy buoy which I knew marked a shallow passage across the Sunk sands, and in spite of the lowness of the tide I believed I could get across, and save some miles. So on a bearing of the Barrow Deep lightship I made for this passage, and immediately the crew of the Edinburgh lightship, who were lined along the bulwarks of their vessel watching my manoeuvres with some interest, ran up the flag hoist JD, or in other words, 'You are standing into danger'. 'Damn 'em,' I thought. 'Do they take me for a fool?' Apparently they did, for when I paid no attention to their signal they fired a gun at me, which had the effect of hardening my resolution, and I carried on. For one sickening moment the strong ebb swept me off my bearing of the Barrow, and my heel caught in the sand while the tide boiled round me. But I remembered some of the lore that five years of cruising in the Thames had taught me, and with the help of the engine kept her nose to the tide so that it could sweep the soft sand from her keel, and gently, ever so gently, she slid into the deep water of the Barrow Channel. And I am prepared to swear that the ship turned round to smile at me as the lightship hauled down the warning signal.

Here at last was plain sailing, plenty of sea room, no wind at all, the engine chugging away cheerily, a bright summer sun, and oh, dear heart! — the end of the search in sight at last. There was still enough of the ebb left to take me down to the Light Float that marks the outer end of the Barrow Deep, and then Harwich would be very near.

I forgot I was tired, hungry, jaded, dirty and unshaven. With the helm lashed a trifle to port she would keep her course for a little, as long as I kept an eye on her, so that I could potter round the decks and remove some of the travel stains that had accumulated during the past two days.

By 11 a.m. I was off the Barrow Deep light float, and even as I passed she swung to the flood. But I slapped the old ship's side and spoke comforting words to her and told the engine that, hard-case sailing man though I was, she was truly one of God's creations made to comfort weary mariners in distress. The sides of the one beamed at me as I rubbed them down with a 'shammy' and the other purred soothingly in sympathy. Seeing they understood me so well, I begged of them that out of the goodness of their hearts they might give me a chance to go below and clean and shave, if only for the sake of common decency, but they would have none of it, and warned me again and again that they were only ready to do their part as long as I faithfully did mine. So, the flood gathering strength, we struggled against it until here was the N.E. Gunfleet, and again I saved a bit of time and an adverse tide by cutting across the head of the sand and laid my course for the Stone Bank buoy.

I do not know much about the experiences of other people cruising, for they invariably navigate their ships with an accuracy and certainty far beyond my powers. Buoys appear and disappear for them with faultless precision, but there are some of them I have never been able to pick up until I had reached a point at which they were no earthly use to me. One of these elusive objects is this same Stone Bank buoy. Look and search as much as I chose there was not a trace of it, but when Harwich harbour was open and the Naze was abeam and I made straight for my goal, the exasperating thing chose that moment to appear just where it ought to have been—under my starboard bow.

Now there was a little breeze from the westward and my sails filled for the first time that day. The sunlight was playing on Dovercourt and Felixstowe as I came up the harbour to look for the Guard, and the happy flood reeled us past Shotley Spit. Before Collimer was abeam I had got the mainsail off her and tied up somehow, and the other canvas came in as Pin Mill, tucked away in its beautiful corner, came into view. Now to look for a safe anchorage clear of the numerous yachts; and one was chosen which looked, and was, the best in the harbour. We steamed past it and then rounded up, nose to the tide and the engine running slowly. As we came to the appointed place the engine was stopped and, as the tide began to carry her backwards, the anchor was let go.

The adventure was ended. I had kept my tryst to the minute.

XVII

An Ocean Race

IT IS A GREAT GAME this Ocean Racing. The first to grasp its possibilities was that superb seaman Lieutenant-Commander George Martin, who recognized, as many of us other old-stagers did, that the day of sail was being rapidly ousted by the cheap motor cruiser, and that unless something drastic was done to counteract the attractions of the 'push button, get you there and back at ten knots' sort of amusement, the time was rapidly approaching when a canvas propelled yacht would be as rare as a canvas propelled trading vessel. There is no doubt that at this period, only twelve years ago, the position was becoming serious, as shown by the small number of sailing craft being built, and these more often than not abortions* of the fifty-fifty type, whilst a perfect spate of motor-driven monstrosities was leaving the building yards in an ever-increasing stream.

There was a lot to be said for these vessels. They were very reliable, their engines functioning well in spite of being subjected to the grossest misuse, and the owners expected, and got, a standard of comfort in the saloons and sleeping-cabins to which the hard-case sailing man was a complete and absolute stranger. Of course, it was argued by the conservative sailing men that these motor cruisers were unseaworthy, and so they were in the sense that they could not have lived in a sea that would not have caused the occupants of a five-ton cutter the least anxiety. If their engines broke down they were helpless, but in fairness, let us add, only to the same degree as a sailing yacht that had been dismasted. Thanks to the reliability of their engines and the well-known rarity of bad weather in English waters during the summer, the motor

---

* This was a common and inoffensive usage in the author's day. —Ed

ship was sounding the death knell of sail, which was slow in anything except a strong fair wind; immobile and the sport of tides in a calm; had, on the same waterline length as the motor vessel, much more limited accommodation and very poor headroom, and was much more expensive to build and maintain. The only advantage the sailer could show when considered as a means of transport was a higher degree of safety and a much more comfortable motion in a seaway.

Something had to be done and done soon if the breed of sailormen was not to disappear from off the face of the waters. It had to be shown that there was more in the art of sailing than simply getting from here to there in the least possible time and with the minimum of exertion. Indeed the multitude had to be taught that there was such a thing as the art of sailing, and that the scope of this art was so wide that it was unlikely the average amateur would ever attain perfection in it; that the problems it presented were constantly varying and were of absorbing interest; that this art was the living embodiment of the ad- age that it is better to travel than to arrive; and that arrival under canvas could give a sense of personal achievement more fully and satisfactorily than could be attained by any power-driven passage. At that time there was only one man who had sufficient experience, authority, and literary ability to make a suc- cess of the movement, and, luckily for sailing men on this side of the Atlantic, George Martin was willing to put his back into the fearful labour involved in starting a movement for the renascence of sailing. The success of his efforts can be seen any day in the harbours round our coasts, and in the races organ- ized by the Royal Ocean Racing Club, of which naturally Lieutenant-Com- mander Martin is the Admiral.

One of my ambitions had been to become a member of the Club, but I had been debarred by the rule that in order to qualify for membership you had to take part in one of their races—to prove your metal (or mettle) so to speak. But when you are living and sailing on board your own ship with no paid crew it is not always easy to convince your wife that a holiday apart would be for the good of both of you. Once I had sold our yacht and bought a house there was no longer any difficulty, and I hoped that some kind friend would give me a chance to qualify before rheumatism made me so stiff that I could not step out of a dinghy. Luckily I had in my possession a letter from the owner of *Bloodhound* saying that he expected me to put myself on board that ship at any time convenient to me. I took him at his word and proposed that I should join for the race to Bénodet. The answer came to board the ship the day before the race, and you may be sure that I had no intention of letting her sail without me. I should explain that I had never met the owner, and his offer was dictated purely by courtesy because I had been able to do him a small service by providing one of his crew.

All in good time I presented myself on board the ship, which lay in the Cattewater at Plymouth. I shall not make any effort at describing her. It is sufficient to say that she was having her first season and that she was the product of the best brains on both sides of the Atlantic. She looked everything that a perfect sea-going craft should look, and when I have said that you know that she was a beauty to the eyes as well. An ugly ship is never a good ship in any sense of the term.

The owner was not on board, but he had left word that I was to dine with him that evening at the Royal Western Yacht Club, where all the adventurers were having their last fling before settling down to work. In the saloon were two young men, the Nossiters, who, in the intervals of sailing the *Sirius* round the world, were having a holiday and crewing for the owner. They were both splendid lads, and after a yarn with them I went ashore to lunch and dismiss my wife. On my way back to the ship in a local motor-boat the boatman asked me if I had heard the news about Mr. Harold Nossiter, and when I said 'No', he told me that shortly after I had gone ashore Harold had been seized with an attack of appendicitis and had been hurried off to hospital.

On board I found that the news was quite true, and learned that the owner was beating up for someone to take his place. While I was talking on deck the owner passed the ship about a hundred yards away, waved his stick cheerily, and called out that he expected me at the clubhouse at seven. I promised to be there, but at the distance we were apart I could not distinguish his face and, of course, under my yachting cap he could not see mine at all. It was not surprising that, as I missed him in the crowd before dinner, he had not the faintest idea who was sitting on his right, especially as there was no formality in the allocation of seats. The owner chatted for some time with the man on his left, and then with his usual courtesy addressed the one on his right:

'Are you sailing in the race tomorrow?'

I admitted that in spite of my venerable appearance I was.

'And what ship are you sailing in, may I ask?'

I tried to be as casual as I could.

'I'm sailing in *Bloodhound*. Quite a good ship, I believe.'

The owner's face was worth going a long way to see. 'That's a good answer.'

'Yes, I thought you would like it put that way.'

I have not described the ship, and I have no intention of attempting to describe the owner. He is like his ship—one of the best products of both sides of the Atlantic.

Early next morning I heard the near sound of a voice on deck, and the distant one of a voice at the masthead. If I wanted to fill any useful rôle it was time I got up and had a look round. One hand was at the masthead, eighty feet high, lashing the racing flag in position, while the skipper was getting sail covers off and reeving jib sheets. In my ignorance of the developments of the modern fast cruiser I was as much use as the fifth wheel of a coach, and felt it. Later our racing crew came tumbling on board. They were the Commodore of the Royal Ocean Racing Club as navigator, the Secretary as sail-trimmer, a naval lieutenant as deck-hand, Frank Nossiter as a representative of real ocean sailorizing, the owner's daughter to lend some graciousness to an otherwise graceless crowd, and myself as ballast.

As we jilled about waiting for the first gun the owner asked me to take her for a bit, a kindly way of suggesting that I might be of some use in relieving the helm. To be a good helmsman is a gift, like those of Kreisler and Gordon Richards, granted to few, and one of the greatest disappointments of my life was when I was compelled to recognize that I could never claim to possess that gift. I had not taken the helm for five minutes before I knew that I had hold

of an instrument fit for a master to play with. It was also plain that the helmsman was not of the autocratic importance granted to him in lesser ships, but
that his mind and that of the sail-trimmer must be woven in the same mesh
in order to get the utmost of which she was capable out of the ship. She was
willing enough to do her part, the beauty, but she was as temperamental as a
Hollywood star, and had to be understood as thoroughly if she were expected
to be the leading lady. When the first gun went I handed over the tiller to the
owner, who always took his ship over the line, and thereafter I gave the seconds as they passed from the stop-watch, thinking what a lot I had to learn on
a subject I had previously thought I knew fairly well.

It was a lovely soft Plymouth morning with a little breeze which as clearly
as possible promised that it was just waiting for the start to die away altogether. That it was as good as its promise may be learned from the fact that at
seven that evening *Bloodhound* and her two most dangerous rivals *Latifa* and
Trenchemer were lying to their kedges off the Eddystone to prevent the tide
from sweeping them up the Channel. But at sunset there was a little westerly
breeze and we got our kedge and laid a course to pass to windward of the lighthouse. As we brought it abeam it seemed unreasonably close, and when two
of the keepers, who were fishing at the base of the structure, began to sema-
phore to us, we wondered whether we were not too close for safety. So while
the lieutenant read the message the navigator took a sextant angle, and the
results were read at the same moment: 'Over half a mile off.' 'Wish you luck
and a pleasant voyage.' Somehow I can never read the latter message without
believing the sender really means it, which is more than can be said for most
of the formal expressions of goodwill.

What did we do for the rest of the night? Well, we slept and we ate and
we worked the ship a little. The owner told stories. The Secretary was possessed of a demon of unrest; he calculated the trim of the sheets in fractions
of inches; he borrowed (having a Scottish ancestry like myself) pennies
from the lieutenant, who seemed to have received the last instalment of his
pay in that modest coinage, and bought penn'orths of wind by tossing the
coin into the water towards the direction from which he wanted the breeze

to come. At times *Bloodhound* responded handsomely to his efforts, but the time came when he recognized that he was buying wind on a falling market, and he went below to do everything possible to show his anguish except tearing his hair.

Bloodhound turned completely round a couple of times after dawn, just like an old dog in the straw of his kennel, and then went to sleep for the rest of the day. In the saloon we all told one another, when we got a chance of putting our oar in, untrue accounts of reputed awful incidents in our sailing careers, as is the way of fishermen and yachtsmen all the world over. The only exception to the storytelling was the Commodore, who had no tales to give, and as an Othello was a hopeless failure. He is a man who tells you his age and then allows every movement of his body and mind to shout out that his statements are not to be trusted. On occasion he will disappear from the haunts of men, and the next news is that he has been heard of somewhere half round the world in a forty-tonner, but you can never get him to tell you a word about it. He never seems to have any adventures, and I often wonder whether it is thinking makes them so with the rest of us. I knew from other sources that he had been in a tight corner on one occasion, and I did my best to get particulars. I noted them in my mind for future guidance, and I think my readers deserve to benefit from the knowledge that was only granted to me as the result of much patient questioning. 'We were all right. You see we had plenty of sea room.' The practical application of this information is still puzzling me. But you can take the positions he gives you as gospel.

During the whole of the day we drifted, and could see the other competitors in the same predicament. If you teased her *Bloodhound* started circling, but if left alone she kept her nose approximately in the desired direction. So we watched the sails of French crabbers and tunnymen in the horizon and felt that it was good to be alive and at sea. At nightfall a little breeze got up and soon we could make out the lights of Ushant thirty miles away, and far astern the loom of the Lizard and the Bishop were seen in the sky. Slowly we worked our way round Ushant and at breakfast we were bearing down on the Ar Men buoy. This wind was almost certain to die away so a course was laid for Penmarch, keeping well outside the indraft into the Raz de Sein, and all that forenoon we sailed pleasantly and quietly along.

As we approached the Raz there was excitement as we recognized *Latifa* anchored inshore to prevent her being carried through the race backwards. She had managed to keep ahead of us since leaving Plymouth, and we chuckled a bit at our cunning in avoiding the trap which had allowed us to overhaul her. But it is a wise resolution never to chuckle at sea in a sailing ship. The west wind died away and left us becalmed, a fresh breeze came off the shore, caught *Latifa* at once, and there she was streaking for Penmarch at nine knots while we wallowed in the swell for another half-hour. As there were only six of us in the afterguard there were only six different ideas as to what we had done wrongly, but over the evening cocktail we agreed that it was all the fault of that adjectival wind for playing a dirty trick on us. However, we got the wind as well and chased *Latifa* past the rocks of Penmarch and down towards the Basse Jaune off the Glénan Islands, where we were to beat up the channel to the finishing line at Bénodet off Combrit point.

We reached the Basse Jaune just as it became quite dark; rain was beginning to fall and the plentiful lights began to appear and disappear in the way that assures you there are plenty of dense patches of fog about. It looked like being exciting work, finding our way up in the dark in an irregular channel sprinkled with rocks. The navigator spread out the biggest chart he had, and with parallel rulers, dividers and pencil, prepared for the worst that the people who were taking bearings could do to him.

A glance at the chart will show the difficulties in navigating this rock-bound, dog-leg channel. With a profusion that is the envy of every British yachtsman the French Government have provided for every need of the navigator, but not even they can help you when the buoys and lights are invisible. In that case you can do one of two things: either you can heave-to in deep water clear of all dangers until the weather is favourable, or you can summon all your seamanship and skill, aided by lead, log, and lookout, and find your way up the channel. The success of this latter proceeding depends entirely on the pilotage ability of those in charge. And here is one of the benefits conferred on the yachtsman by ocean racing. Be sure that heaving-to is going to lose the race for you—if you are not competent to carry on it may be taken for granted that one of the others will tackle the problem with every prospect of success and snatch the victory from you. Given a good navigator this channel can be traversed with reasonable safety, though probably not with the same speed as in clear weather. In this way ocean racing develops the most interesting branch of sailing—pilotage in difficult waters.

We started to beat up. On the chart our navigator had marked out our first course, and any deviation from that course on account of shift of wind was immediately reported and allowed for, so that starting from a known point off the Basse Jaune the distance we could travel in safety on that course was laid down, and as soon as the distance was run the ship was put about and the next course calculated and followed in the same manner. We knew the tide was with us and would be favourable until about three a.m., and the estimated amount it was pushing us to windward was allowed for by the Commodore on the chart. There were two snags we had to beware of, one being that at slow speeds a log is notoriously unreliable, and the other that the influence of the tide cannot be accurately calculated.

Of course we were not entirely at the mercy of our dead reckoning. The fog was careering about in isolated masses and lights would appear and disappear before their periods could be recognized and a bearing taken. Naturally in the haste necessary to get the bearing before the light disappeared in the fog, mistakes were common and a wail from the navigator, 'That last bearing must be wrong,' alternating with, 'For Heaven's sake get me something to cross it with,' came up from the chartroom at frequent intervals. Near lights were invisible and distant ones shone with unnatural brilliance. At one time we had been puzzled by the flashes of a light away in the north-east, and several attempts were made to time it without success until the Secretary was able to say definitely that it was Loctudy. 'Then where in all the world is Île aux Moutons?' demanded the navigator. 'It must be pretty close to us.' We gazed helplessly in the direction it was supposed to be but saw nothing until there was a yell from the helmsman. 'There it is, right over our heads; lee ho,' and as we came round and stood away on the other tack, high up in the heavens we could see something like the moon seen behind thick clouds. We had been within half a mile of this powerful light and had seen nothing of it, while an inferior light over ten miles away had been easily recognized.

Shortly after this the fog cleared away for a little and gave us a view of Combrit point and the lights of the French destroyer off it marking the finishing line. We could not see *Latifa*, but we knew that she had a smart navigator on board and was a few miles ahead of us. She had to allow us a certain amount of time, being a much bigger ship, and the doubt was whether we were going to save that time. The Secretary gave up his strenuous efforts at sail-trimming for the time being when we heard a gun from the destroyer, undoubtedly announcing that *Latifa* had crossed the line. With the aid of x and y and reams of foolscap, he toiled away at the complicated handicap formula and announced that, as far as his scattered wits could tell, we had four hours to do the remaining four miles in order to save our time. And then we all relaxed except the navigator, who had unpleasant things to say about a falling wind and a tide that in a few minutes would turn against us. We hardly listened to him. In our hearts we believed that the cup was as good as in our pockets. It was absurd to think that *Bloodhound* could not do four miles in four hours.

Well, she didn't do it, and how she ever did the distance at all in the conditions which prevailed during the next four hours or so was a source of wonder to all on board. We lost the cup by the narrow margin of twelve minutes.

The hospitality of France is unbounded. We were dined and wined, driven all round their beautiful country, and as a last gesture the night before we left for home there was a dance at the Kermor hotel. I had been standing watching the dancers when a little French lady who had been one of our visitors on board earlier in the day came up and smiled at me. 'Will not monsieur dance with me?' 'It is very good of you to take pity on me, mademoiselle, but I do not dance. I am much too old.' 'You are old, yes. But the heart is young.' Alas for the power of suggestion. For a second I drew myself up and the years slipped from my shoulders. The bufferings of unkindly fate and the kindly seas were forgotten and I was twenty-three again with the world for my oyster.

But the mere act of standing erect gave me a reflection in a mirror over her shoulder, and I came to earth again as a more suitable candidate came forward for the lady's favours. I bent low and kissed her hand. 'Mademoiselle, you are one of God's great gifts to men, but the heart, the heart is no longer young. Good night.'